Book reviews from not- necessarily-famous, but definitely wonderful people just like you

"I'm an avid reader of spirituality books. This book is one of the most amazing books I've read, and I found it to be truly unique. It made me feel really hopeful that I could make deeper, lasting changes with ease, fun, and joy. It makes the typically lofty and philosophical more practical, the complicated easier, and makes real change and growth accessible. It's going to change peoples' lives. I loved it!"

Dr. Annie Jackman, Network Energetics

"This book came into my life when I really needed it, as I was dealing with some big life challenges. The strategies presented and the guided meditations allowed me to shift from feeling overwhelmed to feeling calm and resourceful, and I was able to see positive options and feel joyful again.

Ann writes with an easy clarity. Reading her book is like having a great conversation with a good friend who knows how to hone in on what is most meaningful, essential, and useful. She gently guides us back to what many of us know and feel in the deepest reaches of our being, but what is so easy to lose sight of in our daily lives – who we really are. She skillfully walks us through specific techniques, doorways, to re-connect with the power of Spirit within us, so we can live with more joy, inspiration, ease, and with Spirit perspective. This book is a treasure."

Susan Douglass, Social Worker

"Ann has a conversational writing style that makes reading the book feel like you are working with her one-on-one. In *Three Doorways to the Soul,* Ann does more than present concepts for living from Spirit's perspective, she provides easy-to-follow techniques for making it happen. This book is a gem!"

Beverly Dantz

"I first experienced Ann Ide as a masterful spiritual teacher, workshop facilitator, and coach who helped me expand beyond the small limitations I had imposed on myself. So much improved for me, it's more than I can include here. Having read her new book, *Three Doorways to the Soul,* I know it will be a catalyst for change for its readers. Whether you're a beginner at spirituality or already have a dedicated spiritual practice, this book is sure to open your life up to more ease, joy, and fulfillment.

Written in her signature soft and playful style, the book feels as if Ann is lovingly speaking only to you, and like you're sitting in one of her 8-week programs. When reading the book, I had the awareness that the book had been birthed, co-created with the Higher Source, and in feeling that energy, there was a feeling of "sacredness" every time I opened it.

The book is enhanced with many of her beautiful, guided meditations. Chances are, you will fall in love with her voice and enjoy her meditations long after you've closed the book."

Carolyn Montalto, Executive director,
Community Day Center of Waltham, MA

THREE DOORWAYS TO THE SOUL

From Inner Chaos to Inner Peace,
Living from Spirit's Perspective

ANN IDE

Copyright © 2021 Ann M. Ide

All rights reserved. No part of this book may be reproduced or used in any manner without the prior written permission of the copyright owner, except for the use of brief quotations or references.

To request permissions, contact the author at annide@newpossibilitiescoaching.com.

Paperback: ISBN 978-0-578-88908-5

Ebook: ISBN 978-0-578-88907-8

First edition April 2020

Published by New Possibilities Coaching
www.NewPossibilitiesCoaching.com

Digital book(s) (epub and mobi) produced by Booknook.biz.

Disclaimer: The content of this book is for informational purposes only and is not intended to diagnose, treat, cure, or prevent any condition or disease. You understand that this book is not intended as a substitute for consultation with a licensed practitioner. The intent of the author is only to offer information of a general nature to help you in your quest for emotional and spiritual well-being. The author makes no guarantees concerning the level of success you may experience by following the suggestions and strategies contained in this book. You accept the responsibility for your part in the results you experience and accept that results will differ for each individual. The use of this book implies your acceptance of this disclaimer.

Table of Contents

Index of Guided Meditations	ix
About This Book	xi
Acknowledgments	xv
Introduction	xix
Is this the truth?	xxiii
Why are you reading this book?	xxiii

Chapter One
The Spiritual Solution to Every Problem — 1

What are the fundamental spiritual beliefs underlying this book?	1
How enlightened are You?	3
The Universal Law of Attraction and Tuning In	7
What is the easiest approach to change?	11
Three Doorways to the Soul	16
Recap	18

Chapter Two
Understanding learning and change, so you can be kind and patient with yourself, and others — 21

Four Levels of Learning	22
Five Stages of Learning	23
Moods of Learning	25
The universal cycles of change and why it's useful to know them	29
New Possibilities for You	32
New Possibilities for the World	33
Recap and Practice	33

Chapter Three
Doorway of the Body — 37

- Meditation Made Easy — 38
- Why would you want to meditate? — 38
- Some easy meditation tips and strategies — 45
- How you can easily incorporate meditating into your life — 51
- How being mindful of your body is useful — 52
- What is centering and why is it needed? — 53
- How to Center — 54
- How you can use centering to shift your state — 57
- How you can get better at embodying this valuable skill — 59
- Shifting your body to shift your mind — 60
- Adding connecting to Spirit to the centering process, to "Re-Source" — 60
- Recap — 61

Chapter Four
Holding the Perspective of Spirit Consciousness — 65

- How to ask effectively — 76
- What about all the pain and suffering in the world? — 83
- Summary list of the presuppositions of Spirit — 108
- Recap and practice — 113

Chapter Five
"Abracadabra!" I create as I speak! — 117

- The Doorway of Language — 117
- The problem frame versus the outcome frame — 120
- Using the power of intention — 126
- Lastly, here's a helpful checklist for effective intentions: — 130
- The one question that will set you free — 131
- The difference between fact and interpretations — 133
- The "Is it True?" process (The one question that will set you free) — 136
- Recap and practice — 140

Chapter Six
Your Doorway of Emotions — 143

    Do not bypass your feelings. Listen to them. — 144

    Tips for how to talk about what you want and telling your new believable story — 145

    Heart Coherence — 151

    Recap and practice — 156

Chapter Seven
Using all Three Doorways of your Soul With the Emotional Freedom Technique/Tapping — 161

    How a basic EFT sequence works: — 162

    Tips for wording — 168

    Using tapping to return to your Spirit-Self perspective — 171

    Sample tapping script for feelings of urgency, panic, anxiety or overwhelm — 173

    Using EFT/Tapping to shift a limiting belief — 177

    The process for shifting from small-self beliefs to beliefs held by Spirit — 180

    Sample process and script for shifting a belief of your smaller-self to one of Spirit's perspective — 183

    Recap and practice — 187

Chapter Eight
Putting it all together and next steps — 189

    "I don't like how I'm feeling. What do I do?" — 191

    Tapping integration and review script: — 195

About The Author — 203

Index of Guided Meditations

Below is a list of the recorded guided meditations and exercises, the Spirit perspectives slides, and a Tapping/EFT demonstration video that accompany the chapters in the book. *For the most current, active links, go to www.newpossibilitiescoaching.com/three-doorways-to-the-soul-book.html.*

Chapter One: The Spiritual Solution to Every Problem
- One with the Universe: All the way out, all the way in

Chapter Two: Understanding Learning and Change
- The Space of Stillness and Quiet and gratitude

Chapter Three: The Doorway of the Body
- Meditation Sampler
- Box into Spirit and "Re-Sourcing"

Chapter Four: Holding the Perspective of Spirit Consciousness
- Slideshow with images and summaries for all of the Spirit perspectives in the book
- Guided exercise for practicing the perspectives of Spirit
- I am here

Chapter Five: "Abracadabra!" I create as I Speak! The Doorway of Language
- I am the space for
- Getting a different perspective

Chapter Six: The Doorway of your Emotions
- From chaos to heart coherence process
- Changing your story from inside the vortex of love and Spirit's perspective

Chapter Seven: Using All Three Doorways of your Soul with the Emotional Freedom Technique/Tapping
- Tapping Demonstration Video
- Tapping meditation on feelings of urgency, panic, anxiety or overwhelm

Chapter Eight: Putting it All Together and Next Steps
- Guided tapping meditation for integration and review of all the main concepts in the book

About This Book

Perhaps you've heard that Einstein said that you cannot solve problems from the same level of consciousness from which they were created. The intention of this book is to help you shift from being stuck in the consciousness of your conditioned, automatic, smaller, human mind, to the consciousness of Spirit/Source/God. It will teach you how to solve whatever problem you're experiencing, how to create, and how to live more predominantly from the level of Spirit Consciousness, rather than your more automatic, fearful, reactive self. Having your Spirit Consciousness readily available to you is the most direct and powerful path towards living with all the inner peace, abundance, love, ease, and joy you desire.

I personally consider this to be the ultimate learning of all life's learning, and the one with the most positive impact in every area of your life. It takes place over time, in layers, as you gradually gain more and more clarity, learn more effective practices, and *use* them.

Even though it can seem challenging at times, when you learn to hold a higher perspective, it can all be a grand adventure, like the joy of playing a hard sport or game, AND, with the right practices as well, it can be easier.

By using the strategies taught in this book, here's what past participants in the Three Doorways to the Soul program reported, and what's possible for you.
- "Challenges feel lighter and get resolved more easily."
- "I now experience less stress, even in the midst of challenges, and live more of my time in inner peace and joy."
- "Instead of using forced willpower and discipline, I act more from authentic inspiration."

- "I feel less at the effect of my emotions and circumstances, and seem to have greater choice about how I feel."
- "Instead of getting stuck in emotions that don't feel good, I now embrace them as Divine guidance and use them to shift to an empowered state that feels really good!"
- "I have more energy and health!"
- "My relationships are going more smoothly and are filled with more love."
- "I feel more safe in life, and more confident that I can transform any experience that arises, and create what I desire."
- "I'm manifesting what I want more easily, including abundance, and I'm having more FUN!"
- "I can confidently say, I have never felt as happy, fulfilled, and personally powerful as I do today."

Here's some of what's covered in the book:

- How to easily connect to and feel the energy of the unified field of Spirit/Source Energy/the Universe/God
- Your Three Doorways to the Soul. Each doorway provides indicators of whether you are thinking, feeling, and acting from only your "small", human self or your greater Spirit-Self. And, each also provides the means for shifting your experience, and returning to your Soul perspective, like stepping through doorways. You'll learn strategies for each doorway.
- The Universal Cycles of Creation and Growth, how they impact you, and how to act accordingly
- The many perspectives, or presuppositions and beliefs held by Spirit Consciousness/Source Energy. The better you understand these, the easier it is to return to them.
- How to reveal the more limiting beliefs that are running you unconsciously, and how to transform them to the more empowering beliefs of your greater, whole, Spirit-Self. *The main focus of the book is to expand your way of being in this way, by creating change at your levels of identity and beliefs.*

- How to use language that is aligned with your Spirit-Self, and supports creating what you want instead of what you don't want.
- Tapping (the Emotional Freedom Technique, or EFT) to shift your emotional states and beliefs that don't serve you, into higher, more enlightened states. We'll be integrating Spirit perspective into the normal EFT process to amplify its positive effects.
- Mindfulness strategies that alert you when you're not in the flow of Spirit and can bring you back.
- Heart coherence for receiving guidance and reconnecting to your Wholeness.
- Strategies to use when you slip back into "smaller" ways of being, so you can easily step through a doorway to your Soul and be your whole Self again.
- And, guided meditation recordings are available for each chapter to further support your learning. You're sure to finish feeling good every time, and will also learn a good variety of user-friendly, easy meditation strategies.

Acknowledgments

This is probably the hardest part of this book to write; because how can I possibly acknowledge and thank all of the people who have contributed to my growth and learning, and thus how this book came to be? If you know me or have taken any of my programs, I want you to know that I truly value how you most definitely contributed through our unique experiences to who I am today and the development of this book. Thank you!

I have been so fortunate to have personally studied with real masters in the field of NLP (Neurolinguistic Programming) and with so many of the contributors to the field, such as Leslie Cameron-Bandler, David Gordon, Steve and Connierae Andreas, Lynn Conwell, Robert Dilts, and Tim Halbom and his team. And thank you to Mel Bucholz, hypnotherapist and teacher extraordinaire, who taught me how to access and trust the infinite wisdom of my unconscious mind and consciousness, itself. A huge thank you to Stephen Josephs, for mentoring me so personally and expertly, and taking me on as an apprentice and then one of his NLP trainers. To Marilou Seavey, thanks for supporting me as my first NLP teaching partner, and for allowing me to participate in your Silva Mind Method program. And I have so much love and appreciation for all the dear friends in our weekly NLP study group during those years and all of the deep work we did together.

I was also very fortunate to have studied under Fernando Flores and Julio Ollala, from whom I learned about Ontological Design and many of the linguistic distinctions for being effective in one's life, some of which are in this book.

Other teachers and coaches who added significantly to my spiritual growth through their books and programs, and whose teachings made their way into this book: Deepak Chopra, Joe Dispenza, Esther Hicks and "Abraham", the Ortner family and the Tapping Solution, Sonia Miller, Allison Phillips, Morty Lefkoe, and Elizabeth Purvis.

A big thank you to Maggie Sky and Karen Kuhl and their Roots and Wings Healing Arts Center, who provided such a beautiful, love-filled space for us to lead our in-person programs, and who so generously allowed me to lead meditation classes for free to the public for so many years.

To my Conscious Community meetup, thank you for being a spiritual playground and a place for me to continue to refine my work.

To all of my private and group coaching clients, who were often a mirror for my own growth, who brought great meaning, purpose, and joy to my life, and through which this work was continuously developed and refined. I grew to love each of you and thoroughly enjoyed our work and growth together. This book would not exist if it weren't for you.

To my dear friends who have been on this spiritual path with me: Dr. Annie Jackman, Paul Dolman, Carolyn Montalto, Susan Douglass, and Beverly Dantz; I love you, and so appreciate how you supported and inspired me all these years, for the hours and hours of deep, meaningful, satisfying conversations we had, and for the support and feedback you gave me on this book.

To my parents, Bill and Vera Clenott, thank you for giving me a life in which I felt fully loved, safe, nurtured, and intellectually stimulated, so I could freely explore who I am and my purpose for being. And thank you for all of those years at summer camp, where I developed and enjoyed my connection to nature and Spirit. It was probably far more significant than you imagined.

To my children, thank you for putting up with all the hours I spent working out of our home, for respecting my needs for quiet and concentration, and for bringing more love and joy into my life than I was ever able to imagine.

And most of all, to Mark, who has been my best friend, soulmate and playmate, my husband and New Possibilities Coaching partner, and my in-house, on-demand spiritual guru and coach: There are no words that can adequately express what you mean to me and how you contributed to my learning and growth, to each program we designed and led together, and to this book. You know I couldn't and wouldn't have done it without you. This book is dedicated to you.

Introduction

What's the story behind this book?

I've always been a deep thinker, with lots of questions. As early as my preteen years, I somehow felt like there was more to us than we typically experienced or were taught; and that we were only using a fraction of our potential. I also loved teaching. As a kid, I played "school" a lot with my younger brother, with me always being the teacher. The role I came here to play in this lifetime was clearly showing itself with the interplay of all these factors.

Skip ahead to my early thirties, when my limited beliefs in who could love me got me tangled in a very stressful, long-term relationship. I decided to go to a hypnotherapist for help, and from there, I really took off.

The hypnotherapy sessions fueled my long-standing curiosity about our subconscious, and how we could work with it to expand beyond what used to seem like such fixed personal beliefs and characteristics.

From there, I studied more about hypnotherapy and immersed myself in getting trained and certified in Neuro-Linguistic Programming, the study of subjective experience and how we each uniquely create our experience of reality. It's like understanding a person's unique software programming that creates how and why they think, feel and behave as they do. And, with this deep level of understanding, desired change is easy!

During this period of training, I learned to let go and trust that what I needed to ask, say or do to help facilitate desired changes for someone would show up. I learned how to tap into what I thought at the time was the resources of my mind where all of my training and learning were "stored". Now, however, I know it was much more. I was learning how to tap into my connection to the field of Spirit, and to allow it to speak, flow, and work through me. Although it had never been done before, I was asked to become a training assistant at the institute where I was certified, and a year later, to become a trainer. The power of this Spiritual connection was at play, but I wasn't quite aware that's what it was. It's a good example of how our paths can unfold though.

Over the years, I coached people privately and also led group programs to help people resolve what was troubling them and to find greater inner peace and happiness. Many of these I taught with my husband, Mark; which is why I will say "we" at times in this book. To name just a few of the programs, we had our New Possibilities Group Coaching program, our Living on a Higher Vibration program, and the From Inner Chaos to Inner Peace: Mindfulness, Meditation, and Strategies for Feeling Good program. I had an extremely high success rate at helping people accomplish what they wanted through our work together, typically in a matter of 12 sessions or less. Could this work get even better, even easier? Turns out, yes, it could!

As I began to explore and perceive life more and more through the perspective of Spirit (more on all of this in the book) and to integrate this with the best of the other strategies and processes I'd already been using, it became even easier to resolve my own issues when they showed up, and to move from undesirable feelings to authentically feeling good again, sometimes even better. And, life, in general, got easier and better and better, too!

So, I began incorporating spiritual perspectives into my group coaching programs and my coaching work with private clients; and they had the same positive results, as well. This evolved into our Doorways to the Soul: From Inner Chaos to Inner Peace program, from which this book is based. It has been a most beautiful integration and culmination of the many disciplines and methodologies I've learned over 30 + years, my many years of personal learning and growth, and the evolution of the many group coaching programs I've led. It's time for this to be available to even more people who are open to this and asking for greater inner peace, love, ease, and joy, in a way that is easy to understand and use. I suspect this includes you. I'm so happy to share this with you and expect wonderful things for you as you play along. Enjoy!

Is this the truth?

In my experience (you'll hear me use this term a lot), it's the predominant style and recommendation these days, that to sell books and programs, and to seem credible and convincing, you need to speak with authority, as if you're providing "the truth".

In my opinion, at least in the domain of spirituality and personal growth, there is no one truth. We were intentionally created with free will, and we were also intentionally created to be very diverse, each with our own way of exploring, discovering, and experiencing Spirit, and life. It's an all-inclusive Universe.

Additionally, your inner being knows what is relevant for you and your unique journey and experience at this point in time. I encourage you to always be attuned to this. You get to feel out and choose what's true and what feels relevant at this time for you. I actually believe that we create our truths. I speak to this later in the book, so hang in there.
Therefore, I want to share upfront that I do not claim to be providing you with any "truths" as if they are the only truth and you need or should agree with them. It would be against what I believe in to do so. I will be honest, and I will speak *my* truths.

What I will be sharing with you is what I and my husband, Mark, who has been my spiritual guru and New Possibilities Coaching partner, have found to be extremely useful and effective for us, and for the many people we've worked with. You get to choose what you want to try, too. There's no risk here. You can always go back, right? But, I don't think you'll want to.

Why are you reading this book?

Do you have a library full of books for personal growth of some nature? If so, which ones truly made a lasting positive difference for you, and which ones just became more information to add to your knowledge bank?

I want this book to empower your transformation, and to help you experience greater inner peace, love, ease, and joy *no matter what circumstances are going on*. To do so, we need to partner in this. I'll be the guide if you'll participate by actively engaging with my suggestions. Take your time! A few more minutes of thinking or trying an exercise won't delay your desires. In fact, taking the proper time and attention could expedite your fulfillment!

Of course, you don't *have* to. You get to choose the impact you want this book to have on you. In my experience, what I'm offering in this book is an invitation to something really grand. And, I believe you deserve this.

Let's begin by getting clear on why you're reading this book. After reading each question, take a moment to reflect and actually answer the question.

1. What would you like to change or improve upon in your life?
2. What would you like to experience instead of that?
3. What's your predominant mood throughout your day?
4. Is there a mood you would prefer to experience instead?
5. Does your day flow with ease, or does it too often feel "hard" or stressful in some way? Which is your preference?
6. If you meditate, or do something similar, like yoga, or run, etc., does it help you to feel good; but as soon as you go back to your "reality", it stops, and you go back to your same old self?
7. What consequences of any or all of the above do you experience? (example's: poor sleep, less focus/ability to work easily, snippy with loved ones, feeling tired, lack of motivation)
8. *Why is investing your time in this book important to you?*
9. If you experience any of the above issues and their consequences, how much longer are you willing to continue to experience them?

No worries, I know that whatever you answered, you're not alone. That's why this book came to be. And, I also know from experience with all the people I've worked with for over 30 years, that whatever you desire is easily possible.

Some of what we cover in this book may be something you've already learned from someone else, and I encourage you to let that be very okay. Repetition can be really helpful on the path of mastery, especially for the kind of Spiritual expansion we're here for, since it can be so easy to be pulled into the predominant paradigm around us and what we're so conditioned into. One of my main intentions is to simplify all of this. I hope you'll appreciate this, as well.

Lastly, and very importantly, I designed this book, like I design my programs, with each step building upon what we've done previously, to help you develop more and more emotional and spiritual "fitness" and competencies. *For this reason, it's really best for you if you read the book in sequence.* By the end, there's a beautiful coming together of all of it.

Ready? Let's do this!

CHAPTER ONE

The Spiritual Solution to Every Problem

- The Spiritual paradigm underlying this book
- The three levels of consciousness on the path towards spiritual enlightenment, so you can explore where you are on the spectrum
- The Universal Law of Attraction and tuning in; and what I believe is the spiritual solution to every problem, and the easiest, most direct, and empowering means towards transforming an undesirable emotion to feeling good and allowing what you desire to manifest
- The six levels of experience and change, and the easiest approach to change
- Three Doorways to Your Soul, so you can have a greater awareness of who you're being and have easier access to your greater Spirit Self

What are the fundamental spiritual beliefs underlying this book?

In 2004, a wonderful movie came out called, "I Heart Huckabees". It's a comedy having fun with a lot of different interpretations of what is going on in reality based on a variety of science, philosophy, and new age beliefs. In the movie, Dustin Hoffman and Lily Tomlin play existential detectives, helping people wrestle with and resolve existential issues in their lives.

In one scene, Dustin is trying to explain Spirit, God, or The Field of Infinite Intelligence to his new client, played by Jason Schwartzman. Dustin pulls out a blanket and asks Jason to help him hold and spread it out between them. Once established, for demonstration purposes, Dustin asks Jason to consider that the blanket represents everything in the Universe. Then, by reaching underneath with one finger and poking the blanket up, he suggests that everything is a byproduct of this Field. He says, as he pokes the blanket in different spots, "This is you. This me. This is a tree. This is an idea. This is an emotion.", and so on. He is suggesting that all arises from Spirit or this Unified Field; and, that everything is connected, and thus all one.

Another analogy used to portray this phenomenon is a wave in the ocean. We can see individual waves rising, falling, and crashing; but each wave is still part of one, immense body of water – the ocean. The wave is still the ocean, yes? You are a wave of the ocean of Spirit.
These are analogies of God, Spirit, and/or the Unified Field, suggesting that each of us is an individual human being, but essentially all *"One with the Universe."*

Modern quantum physicists have now explored the depths of atoms and the depths of space to conclude that at the quantum level (the smallest quantity of some physical property, such as energy, that a system can possess), everything is made of energy and is all part of the same energetic field. We are actually all part and parcel of an infinite space of information, intelligence, and potential!

To elucidate this point, did you know that the human body contains approximately 50 trillion cells, and each cell contains approximately 1 trillion atoms? Did you know that an atom is comprised of 99.9999% empty space and that the .0001% remaining that is observable, is somehow not really there, either? It's an electrical charge that is seemingly popping in and out of nowhere. The profound implication is that everything arises from a field of essentially nothing but potential. As humans, we get to create from this field of pure potential.

This is what I mean by Spirit or God, which I might also refer to as Source or Source Energy, the Universe, the Field, or the Field of Potential and Infinite Possibilities. In this Spiritual paradigm, we also believe that Spirit is more than just energy and potentiality. It's also an unlimited, eternal, intelligent, creative, loving, Universal *consciousness*.

Spirit is not "out there" in the Universe, and you are not separate from it in any way. Spirit is ubiquitous. You are an extension of Spirit, and life is a process of awakening to and realizing this seemingly miraculous potential.

When we experience ourselves as just a wave separate from the ocean, and nothing more, we find it useful to refer to this kind of human experience as being our smaller self, with a small "s". And when we are able to remember and act from our wholeness (the ocean), we refer to that as our greater, or whole Spirit-Self, with a large "S". It's important to remember that you don't actually *have* a smaller and greater self. We are always just Spirit, having this physical experience. However, at different times (most of the time), we *experience* ourselves as just a small human self ("s"). By using the strategies in this book, you'll be able to experience yourself more and more as your whole Spirit-Self.

Some day, I hope this will seem as matter of fact as gravity is to us today. Right now, it might seem like just a crazy idea. But, trust me, science is proving it more and more. It's just not the purpose of this book to go into that. If you feel drawn to know more about the science, I invite you to find it. For me, my heart says, "Yes!"; and that's enough for me. How about you?

How enlightened are You?

The three levels of consciousness on the path towards spiritual enlightenment

There are a lot of models out there for the various levels of consciousness we can experience. Here's a nice simple one that works well for me. *Keep in mind, that none of them are necessarily absolute. It's a spectrum, or a continuum, that you can even move in and out of throughout your day.*

Level one: "**I am human. I am my body.**" This is when you think of yourself as merely human and physical, and you go about your day from that perspective. You only have your physical human resources to make things happen. You also tend to be more aware of your limitations; and because of that, tend to have more fear-based emotions and choices, tend to be more reactive to life circumstances and people, and life feels harder.

Level two: "**I am human, and I have a spirit, or Spirit/the Universe exists.**" You're aware there's something grander; but you only experience it or attend to it periodically, like when you need a break or as a ritual in your life, or going to church on Sundays, or going to a meditation or yoga class or retreat, or getting out in nature because you need it. You also tend to think of Spirit/God/the Universe as something separate from you. It exists, but outside of you. Even if you intellectually believe you are more than human, you still basically *experience* yourself as just human most of the time, and thus experience a lot of those limitations.

Level three: "**I am Spirit, and I have a human body.**" Spirit is the greater part of who you are and what you identify as. At this level, Spirit perspective becomes the predominant way of perceiving and experiencing life. The human life you live is like a play or movie or dream. You are an avatar for Spirit. Your eternal, divine Self is what's real. From this perspective, human issues and concerns are lighter, easier. You're a creator, after all! *Learning to live more from this level is the aim of this book.*

When I was a young girl, I loved playing with my dolls. As I played with them, I became them, experiencing the story I was creating for them. Even though I became the dolls for that temporary playtime, that's not who I really was, right? My true self was the me playing with the dolls; and for the most part, I still knew that while I was playing with them and "being" them.

Did you have something you played that was similar? Maybe you used action figures or stuffed animals. Maybe you liked to play "pretend"; and you became some other fantasy role for a short time. Yet, again, that wasn't who you truly were; and to some degree, you probably still had that awareness that it was still you, playing someone or something else.

Ever have a dream that felt SO real? Until you woke up and realized it was just you having that dream?

All of these are useful analogies for experiencing yourself as Spirit, having a temporary, physical, human experience. You were never actually the doll, or pretend fantasy, or dream. It only felt that way. And it was fun!

As I said, these levels aren't absolute, or linear. We dance in and out, with an ebb and flow. There are certainly times when I feel nothing more than being a physical being, and I act accordingly. It's more likely to happen for me when I'm tired and become less resourceful. But it's a temporary forgetting and not my predominant sense of who I am.

This is a spiritual path of learning that tends to happen over time, with us often regressing before a new level of growth. With learning, it can be a path of more and more, and better and better. We're never really "done" or complete", though. We're never going to live at the 3rd level 100% of the time. We came into this form to have the human experience, expecting to experience contrast so that desire and growth would be born from it. But that contrast doesn't have to be big or painful, and it doesn't have to last long, either. As you get better at this, even though you might have an emotional reaction to something, you'll also be able to be more aware of it, be an observer to it, with curiosity, so that you'll be able to use the emotion as a creative process. So it's a dance, almost like a partnering between your physical-self experience and your non-physical self; and you want it to flow with ease, with your Spirit Self being the lead. This is the kind of mindfulness I want to support you in practicing.

If you're on this spiritual path, you're aiming to live more predominantly from the 3rd level: to be there more often, to slip out less frequently; and, when you do, for it to be short-lived because you're more quickly aware of it and *have skills* to shift back to your whole self again. That part is *really* key.

But why did we, Spirit, even come into human form? I once heard that it was for the experience like a young child has playing a game of peek-a-boo. When you forget who you are, Spirit, and then remember again, it's like that totally delighted, big-smiling feeling the young child has when you go, "Peek a boo! Here I am!"

Perhaps it's also for that amazing experience of learning and growth, and being able to live life newly over and over through us. While writing this, I was visited by a one-and-a-half year-old. She was in our bathroom, which has blue tile flooring; and in her bare feet, it was a slippery and cold feeling, and, obviously, a very new sensation to her. You should have seen how fascinated and delighted she was with it, and for a long time, too! Spirit seemed to be having a wonderful experience newly again. I could see it in her eyes, and feel it.

Through each of our unique human experiences, Spirit also gets to experience the unwanted, through which desire is born, and the oh-so-fun game of creating and manifesting happens. The human experience and creating as a human can be likened to a fabulous movie, just temporary, but great pleasure can be had by immersing in it. Through us, Spirit experiences all of our emotions and growth; and through our creating from our desires, life evolves and the Universe expands. It's a grand adventure! To get a fun taste of this, watch the movie, "Michael", with John Travolta; in which he's an angel getting to return to human form to fulfill a particular mission. Boy did he love pie!

So where do you think you might be on the spectrum most of the time? What's your predominant way of being? Do you experience life predominantly through the perspective of Spirit, or as a smaller, physical being?

★ *A big thank you to Allison Phillips (www.allisonphillips.tv) for sharing this interpretation.*

The Universal Law of Attraction and Tuning In

This book is also based on the Universal Law of Attraction. Understanding these basics is important because as Spirit, you are a creator; and you want to be mindful of these principles that are at work. You are always creating, whether you are aware of it, or not. Being mindful of how aligned you're being with these principles and with who you are as Spirit, will allow you to more easily manifest what you do want, versus what you don't want. And, living from the space, or perspectives of Spirit through the Doorways to your Soul, allows this to happen even more effortlessly.

The basics:
- We live in a vibrational, energetic field of pure potentiality. (The "ocean" mentioned earlier)
- This is the field of Spirit/Source Energy.
- We create within this energetic field with our thoughts; and, we create what we focus on, *whether we're aware of it, or not.*

When you have a desire, the *essence* of that desire- WHY you want it, is automatically created within the field, in a vibrational reality. As the saying goes, essentially, "It is done." (the "essence" of your desire). You will manifest it into your awareness in physical form when your energetic vibration, or frequency, is a match to the vibration of the field that it's in, which is the vibration of Spirit/Source (point two above).

It's like tuning in to the frequency of a radio station. Imagine that you want to hear a certain song and there's a radio station playing it. If you want to actually hear it, you need to tune into the station where the music you want is *already* playing, and then you will hear it! Similarly, you want to be vibrationally tuned in to the frequency of the field of Spirit (the radio station) where your desire is complete vibrationally (already playing).

I believe that any undesirable emotions and experiences you have, such as the ones that may have shown up in the answers to the preparation questions in "Why are you reading this book?", are merely manifestations of your smaller selves' unconscious, conditioned programs, and beliefs that are running you. They tend to be limiting, not aligned with your greater Spirit Self, at a lower vibration, *and, end up creating your reality.* That is the "radio station" you're tuned into.

Some examples of these limiting, smaller-self mindsets might be something like:
- My work is the main source of money for me, and I can only make so much.
- Money doesn't grow on trees. Great wealth is possible for others, but not necessarily for me.
- I have to make things happen. Success, or getting the results I want, takes hard work.
- My body is the source of my energy, and I only have so much.
- Other people should act a certain way, and if they don't, it bothers me.
- I'm not good enough, or worthy of what I desire, and/or of love.

Which ones sound a bit familiar? What other limiting mindsets come to mind?

How do you know when a small self program is operating?

Your emotions let you know. Basically, you won't feel as good as you'd like.

Your Spirit Self will never lower its vibration to match a lower perspective of your smaller self. When an emotion doesn't feel good, it's an indicator of the gap between the small self perspective you're holding, and that of your greater Spirit Self's perspective. You're experiencing that inner conflict or incongruity with your true self, *like static on the radio when you're not quite tuned in to the station. That feeling is like the static.*

This sounds simple enough, yet we tend is to accept our emotions as if they happen *to* us and we're just at the effect of them, and we put up with them until maybe somehow they shift! *We just keep listening to the static!!*

How often do you put up with "static" emotions? I doubt you would put up with static on your radio, though. Right? You think it's time to change this?

In the predominant paradigm of some cultures, like the American culture, when we have emotions that don't feel good, we make ourselves wrong. They mean we must have done something wrong or failed in some way, and we try to get rid of them, or distract ourselves from them. Television, shopping, food, alcohol, and mood-altering substances, including pharmaceuticals, are some popular possible examples for this.

In this new spiritual paradigm, we don't want to deny or bypass our emotions at all. On the contrary, we want to pay <u>more</u> attention to them and to embrace and take care of them in a new way, as guidance from Spirit, and through the love, wisdom, and perspectives of Spirit.

How do you know when you're operating from your whole Spirit Self?

- You feel good!
- You experience more ease and flow to what you're doing, and get desired results more easily.
- You have good energy and feel healthy.
- You feel loving and feel loved, and your relationships go more smoothly.
- You feel grateful.
- Life goes more your way, and you *manifest your desires more easily.*
- Challenges feel lighter, and get resolved more easily. You don't have to work as hard; and, even if you do, it doesn't feel that way.
- You feel more inner calm, instead of stress or anxiety.
- Life is more fun!

Einstein said that you can't solve a problem from the same level of consciousness that created it. If you think about it, that would be the small self mindset, right? Yet when we relax and shift to our whole, greater self, the solutions easily arise.

So there are MANY benefits to staying tuned to the field of Spirit or living in that space.

Now, back to when you're not feeling good. If those emotions are "static" indicators that we're not in tune, because we're not perceiving something from our Spirit-Self perspective, then what makes sense as the easiest way to feel better, AND to create a more desirable reality?

Shift to Spirit's perspective!

Thus, living as your whole Spirit Self, seeing, hearing, and thinking from Spirit's perspective, is the solution to every problem. Because when you're in a higher vibrational state of allowing, and you're "tuned in", the solutions, ideas, and insights you need show up.

What is the easiest approach to change?

The 6 levels of experience and change

Here's another model that also helps to explain how having a Spirit level of consciousness can provide the solution to your problems. I learned it from Robert Dilts, one of the great developers in the field of Neuro-Linguistic Programming. It's called the six levels of experience and change, and they work in a hierarchy. The levels refer to the different ways our experiences are created and organized, and the different ways we can change our experience, as well. As a coach helping someone make desired changes, these levels are significant; as we need to be fully aligned at every level for change to be easy. For the sake of my point, however, I'm going to keep it simple for you; because I just want to illustrate the value of working at the level of Spirit.

The first level is the **environment**. It's the **where** and **when** of your experience. Your environment can affect how you feel, right? You can also create some change by changing your environment. Perhaps you've rearranged furniture, or de-cluttered, or organized your desktop for some desired result. For example, it may have helped you feel differently, or work more effectively. This can be a very basic, simple way to create change; but it's not necessarily going to take care of everything you need.

The second level has to do with **behavior**. It has to do with **what** you are physically doing. This is a very common approach to creating change. To lose weight, people typically try to do so by focusing on behavioral changes, like exercising and changing eating habits. Someone might try to get a promotion by speaking to their boss or taking on new or more projects.

The third level has to do with attending to your **capabilities**, which are the mental skills and internal processes that happen in your mind- **how you think**. These will determine the nature of your behaviors, such as your level of competence, your motivation, your memory, how well you communicate, and so on. Your mental capabilities determine how you perceive and direct your actions.

To follow through on our example of getting a promotion, you might also work at this level by taking a training and improving your skill level. To lose weight, you might learn more about how different foods affect you.

At the fourth level, are your **beliefs and values**. These have to do with **why** you think what you think and do what you do. Values are what's important to you, and beliefs are what you hold as true, or not true. *Beliefs and values are behind every choice you make and influence every level below.*

If you don't believe your diet and exercise plan will work, you'll be less likely to stick to it. If you value the pleasure you derive from eating too much or the wrong foods more than you value your health, guess which will have more pull.

With the promotion example, if you take that training, or ask your boss for a promotion, but don't truly believe you could handle the job or have some doubts of any nature, it could show up in how you communicate during that meeting or how well you do with the training.

I once had a client who resented not getting a promotion, since she had worked for the company for many years. Through our work, I uncovered that she questioned the value she provided for the company, and if she did enough for them. Once I helped her realize that she was providing great value for them, guess what happened? She started regularly getting acknowledged for her work, and she got promoted!

When I helped another client of mine believe more extensively in all the value her business provided for her clients, not only did her sales and retention improve, but one of her investors decided to gift her the money rather than have her pay it back.

The fifth level of **identity** has to do with your beliefs about yourself and **who** you are, and your sense of purpose. Do you think of yourself as a valuable team member at work? Do you consider yourself a leader, or just a performer who follows instructions? Do you think of yourself as Spirit, or as only a physical being? Do you consider your body a sacred temple for Spirit to live through, that deserves sacred care? All of these are examples of how your sense of self will influence how you think, feel, and behave. And, how changing your sense of identity can change how you think, feel and behave. It will affect how you stand and walk, how you speak and what you say, what choices you make, and more.

And, finally, at the sixth, highest level, is the level of **Spirit**. This refers to what you feel connected to and believe in that is greater than your human self and to your experience of being part of a larger system, or field. It's above and beyond all the other levels. The more you authentically feel yourself as a part of this unlimited power and everything that comes with that (more on this later), the more you will have all of that available to you. Working with the power that creates all of life is much easier than working to accomplish something through only hard work and willpower!

Can you see how each upper level influences the ones below it? When change occurs at any level, it will have a trickle-down effect on the ones beneath it. You'll have a much easier time achieving a desired goal if you address all of the levels, especially the higher ones. This phenomenon is why people so often struggle with losing weight or any other kind of change. They too often only deal with trying to change the behaviors, without tending to the capabilities and mental strategies available to them, their beliefs and values, their sense of self, and the power that can come from Spirit and its perspectives.

Trying to change from only the lower levels will be slower, harder, and require more discipline and willpower. Whereas when you attend to the upper levels, and especially the Spirit level, the lower levels will more easily adapt to match, and everything will flow with ease. Here again, we have the spiritual solution to your problems, and a much easier approach for experiencing more inner peace, love, ease, and joy.

So, how do you do that? How do you begin to live more from your greater Spirit Self, instead of just your smaller, physical self?

Intellectually understanding this concept doesn't seem to be enough. Even setting the intention to live from a place of Spirit more often doesn't seem to be enough. Have you already done that? Even meditating every day, or going on long retreats doesn't seem to be enough. I've heard from SO many people who do those things, yet still struggle in their lives. They go to yoga or meditate, or a retreat or workshop, and they feel truly great afterward. But, as soon as they go back into their normal day-to-day stuff, they return to their reactive small self at the effect of their outer circumstances. Sound familiar to you in any way?

There have also been trends for some time now to create vision boards, or to visualize what you want and how it will feel, and other similar processes to utilize the law of attraction principles and the creating powers you have as Source Energy. These can certainly help. However, I believe that allowing what you want to manifest doesn't necessarily happen from just these infrequent moments in time.

Living a life of your desires fulfilled comes from predominantly being tuned in to the field of Spirit, where your desires are done (the "radio station" you want to be tuned into). And, for this, you need an expanded awareness of where you're coming from, or who you're being- what identity you're operating from ("s" or "S") moment to moment; and if the "static" is showing up, to be able to tune back in easily. It's an ongoing process. It's how you live. This kind of awareness is part of what I call mindfulness, and there will be more to add to this later.

You are a very fine instrument of Spirit, and, like a musical instrument, you want to stay mindful of whether you're in tune, or not, and to be able to tune up, so to speak, when needed. Imagine if a musician didn't do this with their instrument! If they play every day, I doubt they wait for a once-a-week tuning class to tune up their instrument. I'm not saying that classes and meditating aren't useful. They certainly are. I just don't think they're enough.

What I've found missing for most people, are the awareness and capabilities for what it *feels* like to be their identity as Spirit, what *beliefs* match those of Spirit, the *awareness* of whether they're operating from just their smaller self or their greater Spirit-Self in the present moment; and, when they're being "small", *having some strategies for reconnecting and tuning back into their Wholeness, their greater, whole, Spirit-Self.*

It's just like when a musician hears in their awareness when their instrument is out of tune; and how you notice right away when you're getting static on a radio station and need to adjust the dial (if you had a non-digital model). Being able to live throughout your day from this type of mindfulness and with these skills will set you free. As you proceed through the book, if you follow my suggestions to make this experiential for you; you'll be developing and reinforcing all of this through three doorways to the Soul.

Three Doorways to the Soul, so you can have a greater awareness of who you're being, and have easier access to your greater Spirit Self

What do I mean by Soul?

For some people, the word Soul represents each of our own unique, personal expressions of Spirit. I agree with this, for the most part.

However, for me, from the belief system that everything is Spirit, our Soul *is* Spirit. Perhaps it's a unique extension of it, but it's still Spirit.

Therefore, in the context of this book, when I use the word Soul, it is synonymous with the words Spirit, or God, or Source, or Source Energy, or the Universe, or the Unified Field. I'm referring to the spiritual, non-physical part of you that is infinite and eternal. From our earlier analogy, the Soul is the ocean, and your human physical experience is the wave. It's as simple as that.

A "doorway to the Soul" is thus a doorway to Spirit, a way for connecting to that aspect of you.

Three Doorways to the Soul

The three doorways to the Soul we'll be working with in this book are your body, language, and emotions.

Language includes your thoughts, beliefs, and what you say to yourself and to others. Your thoughts not only create your reality and your experience of it, they also create your vibration. The important question to consider is, are you creating a vibration to match that of your Spirit-Self (the radio station you want to dial into) or a lower one that is denser and matches more to being only physical and human. *So, language is a doorway because how you think and speak will determine if you vibrate at a spiritual level, or not, and what you will physically manifest.*

Your **emotions**, how you feel, are the response to your thoughts; and indicate whether you're vibrating at the level of Spirit or not. They are Spirit communicating to you (doorway) whether your inner narrative and your interpretations that are creating your emotion are aligned with that of your Source-Self, or not.

Your **body** is the vehicle for Spirit to create and experience through, and your vehicle to experience either oneness with Spirit, or separateness through. As it relates to emotions and language, *your body responds to your emotions, thoughts, and vibration; and thus provides another indicator of your vibration, or alignment with Spirit. And, when you're more "in tune" with the vibration of Spirit, you are returning your body to its true high vibrating nature of health and well-being, too.*

Your language, emotions, and body are different, yet they are inseparable. Change in one affects the other, even though you may not be aware of it happening. For example, you can change your thoughts and vibration by shifting your body. Shifting your posture or taking a deep breath changes your body chemistry and changes how you feel and think. The same will happen with taking drugs or alcohol, or overdoing anything, like sports, or eating. The examples are innumerable.

Try this: Slump over in your chair, with slouched shoulders and your head down; and notice how you feel. Can you imagine feeling happy in this position? Now do the opposite, and sit up straight with your head upright and shoulders back. Would it be easy to feel depressed in this posture?

Here's another fun one. Put a smile on your face, even if it's a fake one, and notice how you feel when you do so. It feels more positive, doesn't it? Even without shifting your thoughts first. Now, try to have a negative thought while still smiling. It's pretty hard to do!

Changing your language with the inner dialogue you're having will also change your emotions and your body. Say to yourself, "Here we go with another boring day." How's that feel? Now change it to, "I'm open to delightful surprises today, and looking for reasons to feel good!" Feel the difference?

From the small "s" perspective, you *are* your body, thoughts, and emotions. From the greater "S" perspective, the Soul, you *have* a body, thoughts, and emotions. You *are* the non-physical observer and the creator of what you experience.

It's a really beautiful system, isn't it! And it's all so important if you want to feel good, and have your desires fulfilled. It's ALL about aligning with your Spirit Self by aligning with the narratives and perspectives of Spirit.

Each doorway provides indicators of whether you are thinking, feeling, and acting from your small "s" self or your big "S" Self. And, each also provides the means for shifting your experience, and returning to your Soul perspective, like stepping through doorways. As we continue, you'll learn strategies for each doorway.

Recap

- Everything is Spirit Energy. We live in a vibrational Field of infinite potential.
- Emotions are guidance – indicators of how aligned you are with your greater Spirit Self perspective.
- Emotions that feel bad are like static when we are out of tune with Spirit.
- The Spiritual solution to every problem is to tune into your Spirit perspective.
- Changes at the Spiritual level affect change at all levels below (who, why, how, what, where).
- Your Body, Language, and Emotions are **Three Doorways to the Soul**, with indicators and strategies within each.
- You are a very fine instrument of Spirit, and like a musical instrument, you want to stay mindful of whether you're tuned in, or not.

Guided meditation:

For your first guided meditation in this book, I suggest this very cool **"One with the Universe, going all the way out, and all the way in"**. My intention for you in this meditation is to create a state of awe and wonder, and to perhaps expand your everyday perception of who, or what, you are. For the best sound quality, I recommend you listen to all of the guided meditation recordings with a headset.

To listen to "One with the Universe, going all the way out, and all the way in, go to www.newpossibilitiescoaching.com/three-doorways-to-the-soul-book.html

CHAPTER TWO

Understanding learning and change, so you can be kind and patient with yourself, and others

- Four levels of learning
- Five stages of learning
- Three significant moods of learning and change that either close or open possibilities
- The Universal Cycles of Change and Growth
- New Possibilities for You and the World
- My #1 go-to strategy for connecting to the space of Spirit. "The Space of Stillness and Quiet guided meditation"

With next-day delivery, quick-cooking meals, and so much being available at the click of a button these days, I see a lot of us having developed unreasonable expectations of ourselves, and others. In the domain of learning, I see a lot of us somehow expecting to quickly and easily learn and excel at something, and getting frustrated when we don't. Sometimes we even think things like something's wrong with us, or what we want isn't possible.

You've likely heard that learning is a process. The path of spiritual enlightenment most certainly is! And, I bet there's a part of you that doesn't like hearing this again! "Ugh. I want it to be easy!"

The point of this book *is* to make it *easier*. I believe it's still a process, but it doesn't have to be hard. How about approaching it with joyful anticipation? Have you ever had to prepare for going away on a vacation? There can be a lot to that process: researching places and tickets and purchasing them, perhaps researching what to do, getting things done at work and home so you can be away, packing, and so on. Yet, you do it with a background of, "This is going to be great!", or something similar; and you just accept the process.

Let's do that with this learning. Let's even let it be fun. I also have a few more frameworks from the fields of learning and psychology that most people find very helpful in accepting the process of learning and change. Like the levels of consciousness, you will also experience these on a spectrum. We don't jump from one absolute level or stage of anything. These are just guidelines to help give you some perspective on your experience as you engage in learning and growth in any domain.

Four Levels of Learning

Unconscious incompetence: When you don't even know what you don't know and what's possible, that's called unconscious incompetence. Was there a time in your life that you weren't even aware that there are strategies for managing your emotions and that you don't have to be at the effect of outer circumstances? Or was there a time when the idea of thinking of yourself as Spirit and seeing life through that lens didn't even exist? If so, that was just unconscious incompetence. You just didn't even know.

Conscious incompetence: The next level is when you're aware (conscious) of your incompetence, but you're still not competent. This is called conscious incompetence. Maybe that's how you feel now about your emotional competence, or your ability to create inner peace more often, and why you're reading this book. Again, this can be a frustrating level to be in. However, instead, you could think of it as an opening, an opportunity. It's better than being totally unconsciously incompetent! Right?

Conscious competence: If you take action on your incompetence, and begin to learn what's needed, you then move into conscious competence. You have some competence, but you still have to think about it consciously. It still requires a good deal of concentration and focus on that one task. Maybe you can remember something like this in your life. Can you remember when you were learning to drive? You had some level of competence, but it still wasn't second nature. You had to stay very conscious about it. That was conscious competence.

Unconscious competence: Ideally, we eventually move to unconscious competence. The term "unconscious" here is not used as it is when you hit your head, blank out, and go unconscious. It merely means that your competence occurs on automatic, with barely a thought or any conscious effort required. It's effortless and natural. Examples would be how you probably read now, or how you drive a car, or maybe how you cook or perform some other skill you've developed at work.

As you can imagine, we don't just automatically move from unconscious incompetence to unconscious competence. *It's a process.*

Five Stages of Learning

- **Beginner:** This is the beginning of learning, when you become aware and declare that you don't know, you want to learn, you might seek help, and you begin the process. Let's use the beginning of learning to play an instrument to become a musician as an example.

- **Minimally competent:** Just like it sounds, this is the phase of learning when you're developing a little competence. As you continue, you'll develop a little more, and then a little more, and a little more, until you eventually become competent. At this minimally competent stage, you can play some songs; but you're not ready to perform and have people enjoy it quite yet.

- **Competent:** This is when you've developed the capabilities to experience the results and experiences you desire in a given domain. Now you would be ready to perform well enough for others to enjoy your playing.

- **Virtuoso:** Now you *excel* in what you're doing. To follow our example, you'd be competent enough to get paid at a very good rate for what you're doing.

- **Mastery** – When you qualify as a master, you not only excel, you can also innovate. As a masterful musician, you can go beyond just playing the music provided. You get more creative in your playing, and maybe even do some composing.

When I was a virtuoso coach, I excelled at using techniques I'd learned to get desired results for clients; and as a trainer, I excelled at following the training manual. As I became a master, I began to use all the techniques I'd learned with more creative artistry, mixing and matching and coming up with new adaptations of my own, and doing it all from a space of Spirit coaching and teaching through me.

If you want to develop new habits of thought and new ways of thinking, feeling, and being from reading this book, practice will support you in that goal. The neurological pathways of your automatic, habitual ways are like deeply grooved water channels. Water will tend to flow through the biggest channel- *the one that has been used most*. Your neurological patterns and programs are similar. Your problematic patterns are just very well practiced! You can develop new pathways by using them, so they will deepen like a water channel and eventually become your new normal. And, the old neural network will actually get smaller. You can also think of it as building muscles to become more spiritually and emotionally "fit". Again, this doesn't have to be hard. Just follow my simple suggestions for easy, rewarding results.

Moods of Learning

Our moods as we're living and learning are also very significant. In our teaching, we define mood as an automatic assessment about your future possibilities in a specific context. For example, a mood of resignation comes from an assessment that there are no possibilities that are likely for you. A depressed mood can come from an assessment of feeling hopeless or helpless about achieving or having what you desire.

Moods will influence your ability to experience and accomplish what you want, how you'll feel, and how easily it will happen, or not, including in the domain of learning.

Three significant moods of learning and change that either close or open possibilities

- **Confusion:** When you're in this mood, you're thinking something like, "I don't know what's going on, and *I don't like it.*" It's a mood of not accepting what is, and being uncomfortable with uncertainty. It's often called a "bad" mood. "I'm in a bad mood." This mood limits your possibilities, as it's not very open. Have you ever had an experience of something not going as you'd like or had planned, you're not certain as to why, and you are emotionally suffering about it? How about when your computer isn't functioning as you need it to?

- **Perplexity:** The inner narrative for this is something like, "I don't know, but I have questions." It's being more curious and open-minded, and opens up your possibilities for something different. With the malfunctioning computer example, if you stay in just confusion, it's likely to make the solution a lot more elusive. But when you are open to questions, it opens up the path towards possible solutions.

When I was teaching at Boston College many years ago, I was teaching a program called Learning to Learn. It was created by modeling the mental strategies and thought processes used by successful learners, and we taught these strategies to students who were struggling in the academic context. I would say the key component used by successful learners was having a questioning mind, and mentally having questions throughout the learning process – while taking notes, reading, while writing, and to help organize information.

When you have a question, your mind automatically begins to seek the answer. It almost can't not do that. By the way, what's the weather like today?

Did you notice where your mind went? I'm certain it went right to searching for the answer or trying to make some kind of sense of why I was even asking it. Questions also help you to make sense of and order information; which then helps you to remember it more easily, as well.

So questions are very powerful for learning, for opening up new possibilities, and in helping you get where you want to be. Get into a detective-like state of having questions from a pure, open, non-judgmental, *not-already-knowing* state. To help you get into this state, try tilting your head a little to the side, looking up a bit, with your hand on your chin. Imagine being a detective curiously asking questions, reaching for answers. You don't know the answers YET; but you know they exist!

- **Wonder:** Here we have, *"I don't know, and I like it!"* Like a child with open eyes, full of questions, wonder, and awe, you're engaged with the mystery of life and the unlimited possibilities that can arise from this unattached state. It's like wondering what you're going to get for the holidays. You don't know, but you're excited with eager anticipation! Vibrationally, this is a very allowing state. There is no resistance or blocking of your desires flowing to you. If we go back to our radio analogy, you'd be having thoughts like, "I wonder what I'll find playing!" You don't know what songs will be playing, but it's okay!" If we compare this to the detective-like state of perplexity, wonder would be a detective who had a passion for his/her work and loved the process and pursuit towards the surprise at the end. Like a great game, you don't know exactly how it's going to end, but you still love playing!

I remember when I was starting my coaching and teaching practice, and I had minimal competence at manifesting clients who were looking for someone like me. If I had stayed in a mood of confusion, simply feeling defeated and frustrated with where I was at, it's possible I never would have served anyone. And, I also wouldn't have grown in the many personal ways that I have through the process of being an entrepreneur. Instead, I held a mood of wonder, of, "I'm not even sure what I still don't know, but this is a process, and when I finally get it, and when I break through the limitations being revealed to me, it's going to be great! I'm looking forward to that!"

Notice that all three of these moods begin with, "I don't know." What I have learned and come to accept as true, is that we human beings do not really know the future; that no one really knows the future, no matter how convinced you may be, or how convincing someone else may sound. Yet, somehow, we are all still responsible for creating our future. Some moods support and/or open possibilities for learning and growing. Some moods thwart or close possibilities for learning and growing. Moods like confusion and resignation close possibilities. Moods like perplexity and wonder open possibilities.

Learning and change involve experimenting, making mistakes, getting feedback, self-correcting, and experimenting, and trying the process again. Right? We expect and even support this with children, and they are amazing learners! The amount that they learn in a short period of time is astounding! Their mood of wonder plays a big role in allowing this, too.

Then, for some reason, we start to develop unreasonable expectations of ourselves and others as the age of adolescence is reached. Just because someone is getting older, they "should know and do better". We no longer honor the levels, stages, and moods of learning; and this can get in the way.

My invitation to you is that you move through this book and your learning in a state of wonder and openness, and letting yourself be a beginner. Let it be okay with whatever stage you find yourself in, and just continue playing, maybe making mistakes, getting feedback, self-correcting, experimenting, and committing to the process. Take note of and acknowledge *any* progress, positive changes, and experiences. It will help you to continue to joyfully move forward.

To help reinforce the value of what I've just shared and suggested, read and reflect on the following questions, and notice what answers show up for you:

1. What are some examples in your life of successfully moving through these levels and stages of learning? And, how much time did you allow yourself, or did it take? You might use something you're good at at work, or a hobby you're good at, or a sport, or even something simple that you're good at at home, like cooking.

2. Other than time, what else allowed you to succeed? (what was your process, attitude/mindset, what strategies did you use)

Can you now better understand the value of being kind and patient with yourself, and how remembering these frameworks and distinctions will help you to do so?

The universal cycles of change and why it's useful to know them

We're living in an amazing time. A time of transition as humans evolve from living in a paradigm of life being just matter-based and thinking we're just physical beings, to a paradigm of everything being energy, and that energy being that of an intelligent, loving, creative Spirit Consciousness. But, as I'm writing this, there seems to be a great deal of chaos in the world now. There's political and government chaos, environmental and climate chaos, terrorism ,and mass shootings. I won't go on, as I suspect you're quite aware of what I'm talking about.

I, and many other spiritual teachers, believe that the outer chaos that we're experiencing is actually the cycle of growth and change that our planet and human species are in; and that the world is in a very exciting precipice of growth and evolution right now. Chaos is actually part of the nature of change.

Here's a model that explains this. It can be really useful, and soothing, even.

Kris and Tim Halbom, trainers, developers, and authors in the field of NLP (Neurolinguistic Programming), observed that there are seven phases of change that *all* systems progress through. By all systems, they mean:

- Nature and all living systems, such as in trees, plants, cells, planets, animals, *and humans*
- Non-living systems, like computers, businesses, and educational systems
- The systems within human life and behavior, such as in relationships, health, and personal growth

They call the phases the Universal Cycles of Change, and they claim that people who do well in life are naturally attuned to them. By being aware of what stage you are in, you can more easily accept what's going on, and then, if appropriate, more consciously plan for the next stage. See if you can guess which stage stress would fall into, and what the potential consequences could be if no action is taken. Keep in mind that we go through various cycles in a day, month, year, and lifetime; and that cycles are contextual. You could be in one stage of one cycle in your career, another in your health, and another in your relationship, and so on.

The cycle begins with **Creation.** This is the phase of new beginnings. It might be an idea, or an action, or the planting of a seed. It's the starting point of...

Growth: This is when the "system", which could be you, begins to grow and develop by "self-organizing". New patterns begin to take shape and form. Here you would observe a tree growing branches, buds, and leaves.

The third phase is **Complexity to Maturity.** As the system continues to grow, it becomes more and more complex and mature, eventually reaching a "steady state". This is when things are going really well, and are relatively stable, as in the full bloom of summer.

Eventually, the phase of **Turbulence** sets in. Growth becomes too complex and problems or challenges start to develop. *The turbulence is feedback that something has to change to allow more growth to occur, or even just to return to stability.* This is easy to observe in nature, such as when a forest becomes overgrown, or an animal population too high. In a relationship, there might be more arguing, as differences seem more apparent and less tolerated. In a business, customers might start complaining about services not being delivered satisfactorily. In health, you might start feeling more tired and get sick more often.

If nothing shifts or no changes are made during turbulence, then **Chaos** sets in. Things begin to really fall apart. Turbulence is about the beginning signs of potential chaos. Once in Chaos, things really break down. Someone in a relationship has an affair. In business, good people start quitting, customers and big proposals are lost. People might experience depression of some sort or have constant worry and anxiety, or develop a chronic or serious illness.

Most of us are aware of how nature finds ways to restore balance when it becomes too complex. Forest fires are a dramatic example. *On a more personal level, to move forward through the life challenges of Chaos, we need to let go of or reorganize something.* It might be a relationship that no longer serves you, or a limiting belief, or changing a behavior, or changing your perception of something. By doing this, space or opportunity is created for something new. This is the phase of **Dropping Off and Reorganization.** Most of us have at least heard about a business going through reorganization and laying off a significant number of employees as part of the process. *This is not done merely for the sake of surviving. The intention is to allow for new creation and growth.*

After this phase, almost as a part of the reorganization, there's a period of **Dormancy** while preparing for what's next. In nature, this would be winter, as one example. For people, it's a time of inner reflection, which can show itself in various ways. I remember as a teen listening to music and reflecting for hours at the end of every school day. This is a time to renew and rejuvenate. Sometimes it can be uncomfortable to take the time to do this, rather than move into action right away. But allowing whatever time it takes to do this is usually worthwhile. You'll be all the more prepared to once again move into strong new cycles of **Creation and Growth**, and less likely to make the same mistakes.

Stress = Turbulence

Within this framework, can you see the opportunity that stress and chaos can have for us? The stress you feel is the turbulence – the feedback that your system has become too complex or ineffective in some way for you to thrive and for more growth to occur. If you neglect to make any changes, you will most likely eventually move into chaos and have even more serious breakdowns.

So, should you try to avoid turbulence altogether? Not necessarily. Trying to avoid turbulence could mean avoiding growth and expansion. The key is, as mentioned earlier, being attuned to it before it becomes chaos, seeing it as a part of your life's ongoing cycle of growth and change, discovering what this is feedback for, and finally taking appropriate actions of "Dropping off and reorganizing".

Unfortunately, unlike any other living system, humans tend to resist and/or ignore feedback and change. Our brains are designed to prefer the familiar, because knowing what to expect, if even uncomfortable, feels safer. We deny, and think that we can just dig our heels in and persist in the same behaviors, trying to be strong and do what we believe is necessary. We struggle with the ideas of "dropping off" anything or reorganizing in some way, or getting help, with ungrounded assessments like "I just can't" or "I don't have the time or money" or "It's the wrong time." or something else is more important, and so forth. Everything else seems more important than our health, well-being, and happiness. And, even if we do make changes, they are often in haste, with not enough time taken for the inner reflection of the Dormancy stage. Who has time for that?!!

New Possibilities for You

When you feel stress, or observe turbulence or chaos, acknowledge it as part of a process of something even bigger: as feedback for the potential of chaos, <u>or</u> the potential for growth and something even better than before! <u>You get to choose</u>.

There are a lot of possibilities for letting go and reorganizing:

You can make "outer" changes for designing a life with less stress, such as learning new skills for managing your commitments and capacity.

Outer changes alone are rarely enough, however, even though this is usually what people focus on. You also need to address your "inner" world, such as:

- Changing your beliefs and perspective
- Adjusting how you interpret circumstances and create your stress
- Creating inner harmony and accessing your resources with strategies like centering and meditating and connecting with your whole Spirit Self

We'll be covering these as we continue in the book.

New Possibilities for the World

Can you see now that all the chaos in the world also has the potential for something better? Perhaps we're being led to the necessary letting go of old ways of being, and towards taking on new ways for new growth. Perhaps we need to be patient, open, and curious, rather than angry or resigned or judgmental, as we move through the levels and stages of learning and growth, realizing that changes, and evolution, take time and a process of making mistakes and getting feedback.

I invite you to keep this more positive perspective in your consciousness, not only to alleviate any stress over it; but also to help create something better. We create as we think, after all.

Recap and Practice

As I said earlier, this book is a building process. Each chapter and section builds on the ones prior, to help you develop more and more emotional and spiritual "fitness" and competencies. We'll be deepening those new "water channels".

In Chapter Two, I introduced some valuable frameworks: the levels, stages, and moods of learning, and the Universal Cycles of Change.

Over the next week, set a daily intention to be mindful of your mood. If you catch yourself in one that has some confusion, such as "I don't know what's going on, and I don't like it.", play around with shifting your body (with your head up a bit, or shift your posture, or smile a little) and direct your thoughts into perplexity or curiosity.

You might also *think* you know what's going on. Even then, I invite you to be more in the moods of perplexity and wonder.

Ask some questions *openly*, like, "I wonder how I might think differently about this." or "How could I think differently about this?" or "What could I do to feel better?" or "*What would I say to a good friend about this?*" As we continue, we'll also be discussing more specific ways to shift your inner narratives to better-feeling ones.

You can even just start becoming more aware of which of the three moods of learning and change you're in. That will be a good start. And, what stage of the cycle of growth might you be going through in a particular context?

These things can be done *at* any moment, *in* a few moments, and can still have a significant positive impact, even at your desk at work.

Guided Meditation Recommendation

As we move through our time together, one of my intentions is for it to become easier and easier for you to experience yourself as Spirit/Source, and to have a variety of strategies for returning to it. I like to call this "Re-Sourcing". It's important for all of this to be more than just an intellectual, conceptual process. You want to *feel* yourself as Spirit, as well.

My guided meditations will be great practice for experiencing yourself as Spirit and reconnecting to your Wholeness, and for building a felt sense and body memory of your oneness with Spirit. Consider them like training wheels on a bike, with the goal of you eventually being able to ride on your own. Again, if possible, I recommend listening to them with headphones for better sound quality.

Spirit is *always* present, within and around you, everywhere. What will allow you to experience it is simply a matter of developing and placing your awareness on it.

Place your attention on your toes. Now you're aware of them, right? Before I suggested it, they probably weren't in your awareness, as if they didn't even exist. Put your attention on them, and there they are! Of course, they were *always* there. Same with your greater Spirit-Self. Always there. You just gotta notice, by just shifting your focus.

How it feels will vary greatly each time. Sometimes it will just be a subtle feeling of peace, or something else positive. It can also be so moving that you just don't know what to do with it. And, there can be limitless variations in between. It might just be "hanging out" in the background, like knowing your peaceful, sleeping pet is nearby, and you somehow feel its presence. Or, it can be powerful. It's so varied and so personal, and there is no way that is right or wrong. *The only constant is that it will feel good.*

In **"The Space of Stillness and Quiet"** guided meditation, you'll practice shifting your awareness to where the stillness, peace, and quiet already exist, which is the same as the space of Spirit. This is my #1 go-to strategy for connecting and "Re-Sourcing". This doesn't mean it will necessarily be your #1 strategy; only that I think it's worth trying.

I usually shift my awareness, with my eyes softly open, to sense where the stillness, quiet, and peace already exists in the space all around me. The space of quiet between the sounds, the peace right there in the midst of whatever. I can feel it immediately. It quickly becomes unlimited spaciousness, and the space of Spirit, and my expanded Spirit-Self. I instantly feel that peace and calm. And, since I practice this with my eyes open, I can now easily speak and do things outside of meditation while holding it.

There are so many ways to shift into our expanded Selves; and, it seems to me that it takes form in ways that seem to match our human personalities. In this way, as more of us embody all that we are, we still won't all be the same. It's so beautiful! So brilliant a design!

At the end of this meditation, we also spend some time in gratitude, a very simple yet powerful means for raising your mood, your vibration, and thus "tuning in" to Spirit. Practicing gratitude also helps train your mind and build neuropathways to look for and notice what's good, rather than what's wrong, or missing. It can be a significant life changer for feeling good more of the time.

After listening to these a few times, you can begin playing on your own by simply shifting your awareness to connect and "tune" yourself by finding the space of stillness, quiet, and peace that already exists and is always present in the space around you- the Space of Spirit.

To listen to the Space of Stillness and Quiet guided meditation recording, go to:

https://www.newpossibilitiescoaching.com/three-doorways-to-the-soul-book.html (total time 19 minutes)

CHAPTER THREE

Doorway of the Body

- Meditation made easy
- Being mindful and aware of Spirit's communication to you through your body
- Centering to reconnect to Wholeness
- Guided meditation to practice "Re-Sourcing"

How your body is a doorway to the Soul, and how you can use it

As mentioned before, your body is the sacred instrument through which Spirit gets to create and experience. It is a physical manifestation and extension of Spirit, just like your arm is an extension of your body, thus a part of, and one with your body. Through the sensations of your body, you're given signals as to how in tune your instrument is with your greater Spirit aspect.

Is your breathing full and easy, or shallow and up high in your chest? Is your posture relaxed and upright; or are your shoulders uptight or slumped and rounded? Are your muscles relaxed or tense? Is your heart racing, or normal? Even how you're holding your facial muscles and expression can indicate who you're being. Is your brow furrowed, or are your eyes squinting? Is your jaw tight or clenched at all?

I'm sure from these examples you can imagine and recall your own physical experiences on the spectrum of comfort and discomfort. This happens because, whether in your awareness or not, your body responds to your emotions, which are created by your thinking. And, like your emotions, your body will let you know if your thoughts are matching that of your whole Spirit's perspective, or not. Thus, it's a good idea to do a physical scan regularly throughout your day. When you notice that you're experiencing some physical discomfort or tension, signaling your discord with your Spirit-Self, observe what you've been thinking and what your mood has been like. Be a witness to your thinking, "Oh! I'm having thoughts that don't feel good when I think them." Later, we'll cover strategies for creating better feeling thoughts.

The practices in this section will help to build your awareness of how differently it physically feels when you're being your small self vs. your greater Spirit-Self, your Whole Self. I will also give you strategies through the doorway of your body for tuning in to the field of Spirit, practicing and reinforcing this, and for returning to your Wholeness when needed. First we'll talk about meditation. It's a wonderful vibrational tuning tool.

Meditation Made Easy

Why would you want to meditate?

First, let's talk a bit about why you might want to meditate. There are so many reasons!

You know how you feel when you're ready to stop working, and you're ready to just let go and fully relax? Maybe for you, it's that feeling of getting under the covers in bed and letting out a nice relaxing sigh of relief. Or maybe it's that feeling of settling into a good cup of coffee, tea, or wine – when you're just focused on the goodness of it and a relaxing few moments. Or maybe it's getting comfy for a good TV binge or movie, or with a good book, or sitting by a fire. It's a feeling of letting go of the busyness of doing and thinking, and sinking into comfort and relaxation. It's simply stopping and bringing yourself to calm and stillness inside. It's intentional, and what you do with your body is a big part of making it happen.

Can you relate to any of that? When you allow yourself to do it, it feels really good. Right? To me, this is one significant reason to meditate. When you drop into a space of peace and calm, *it feels good,* and, it's really good for you, too! And, all you need is *you*!

Here are some of the potential benefits shown through studies:

- Can reduce chronic pain, anxiety, high blood pressure, cholesterol, substance abuse, post-traumatic stress response, and blood levels of stress hormones.
- Less insulin resistance- a predictor of future heart trouble and diabetes.
- Improves sleep patterns, reduces inflammation, reverses aging, increases general health and longevity, releases tension, alleviates depression
- Stimulates whole-brain functioning, increasing creativity and mental abilities, focus, and concentration, helps you make better decisions
- Can improve mood stability and make you less reactive

I suppose those alone are pretty compelling reasons to meditate. But, to be honest, that's not what motivates me. Here's what's even more meaningful to me.

When you meditate, regardless of how short or long it is, you are returning to experiencing your Whole Spirit-Self. And, *that's* what feels so good. Meditation itself is not the source of serenity. It's a means to help you become aware again, and experience again, *what's always there,* and who you always truly are.

As you've been reading this, you most likely weren't aware of your toes, even though they were always there. However, if I ask you to put your focus on them (which I already did), there they are again! It's the same with Spirit, and the peace, love, ease, and joy that it is. It's always there and available to you. You just have to become aware of it again.

Meditation is a means for practicing this shift in awareness; and, ultimately, you'll be able to easily shift your awareness in any moment, like re-noticing your toes, to the space of Spirit, and all the possibilities that will open for you.

Through meditation, you're also tuning your vibration (your "instrument" or radio) to everything that the field of Spirit is already "playing" for you: good health, abundance, a feeling and knowing that all is well, peace, love, joy, resourcefulness, creativity, wisdom, solutions, ideas, and better-feeling thoughts that match Spirit's perspectives.

By being more tuned, it will be easier to manifest what you want because you'll be out of the "static" mode, and tuned in to where the essence of your desires are already done.

I also believe that when you meditate, you're practicing how you want to be in the world: present, mindful and calm, experiencing more from your Spirit perspective than your reactive smaller self. Through meditating, you become more familiar with what this feels like; so you become more aware of when you're not being your Whole Self. The more a musician plays their tuned instrument, the easier it is to notice when it's out of tune. It's the same with us.

Meditation is a Doorway for the Soul through the body because you're intentionally using your body to create an inner state of stillness, peace, and calm, and to re-calibrate to your Soul- your Whole Spirit-Self. This will have a positive impact on your body as you do so, as well. Doorways work in two directions, right?

Since the doorways are actually inseparable, there's also a language aspect to meditating. In my opinion and experience, meditation is not always about creating silence within. Meditating is about practicing being the observer of your thoughts, rather than becoming them and having them run you. "I'm *having* these thoughts. I am not my thoughts." is a classic way of putting it. Another useful analogy I've heard is that it's like watching traffic go by. You observe the cars, but don't necessarily jump in and take any of them for a ride.

If a thought feels good, milk it! Even create some more good feeling thoughts to focus on, like thoughts of gratitude and appreciation, or thoughts of love, or imagining what your desire fulfilled feels like. These can be delightful, vibration-raising ways to meditate!

You might also notice thoughts that don't feel good, and through that increased awareness you can change them to ones that authentically feel better. This is useful, too! As the observer, in your raised awareness of what you're thinking, *and how each of those thoughts feels*, you get to choose which ones you want to take for a ride. Having more awareness of and choice of your thoughts is what I consider being mindful, and is a great skill to nurture! We'll be talking more about this kind of mindfulness later.

So meditation isn't necessarily about silencing your thoughts. It's a way of practicing how you respond to them. And, since you create your experiences with your thoughts, you're also learning how to be a more conscious creator of your experiences, rather than being at the effect of circumstances.

There's also the potential meditation provides for receiving guidance and wisdom, such as solutions and ideas that inspire you, and more useful ways of thinking about something.

Sometimes when I begin my meditation, I'm aware of "planning" thoughts, or something I'm needing to process. Ever hear someone say, "I just need it to be quiet so I can think!" If you are, or have been, or have had a parent, I bet you know what I'm talking about. The quiet time provided through meditation can even be a useful time to just process whatever you need to process or think about in a resourceful, generative, productive way. I've even done some meal planning in meditation! You think it's a better time to do this kind of thinking than when you go to bed and end up staying awake? I do.

In his book, <u>The Way of Zen</u>, Alan Watts famously wrote, "Muddy water is best cleared by leaving it alone." Continuing to shake a jar full of water and dirt will only make the water cloudier. The only way to find clarity is by letting the jar sit and settle. Overthinking and analyzing can be like shaking the jar. Your thoughts can get so jumbled that you can hardly see your way out. Sometimes you need to just stop the trying, stop "shaking the jar", and let your mind settle for the clarity, wisdom, and guidance to come."

You see, for everything you think from your smaller self-perspective, the greater part of you, Spirit, has a thought/perspective on it, as well. It's always pure, *positive energy*. So you want to be able to hear that, rather than only your smaller self's thinking. As you quiet your mind and thus allow your vibration to rise, you'll find yourself thinking thoughts that come from Spirit, rather than your small self. They beautifully and effortlessly show up. How this happens will be different for everyone. You might get images, or hear thoughts, or just sense something. Be open to anything. And keep in mind that it can be soft, subtle, or fleeting; but trust it, anyway.

So, meditating gives you time not only to reconnect and attune to your greater Self, but also to *hear its wisdom and guidance,* as well. This is probably my favorite part of meditating, and I even find it fun!

If you'd appreciate having access to any of the wide range of benefits I've just mentioned, then maybe you think it's worthwhile to meditate for at least a few minutes each day.

What meditating feels like, and are there right or wrong ways to meditate?

Meditating can feel like anything that you might feel when not meditating. It's not always a Zen, Buddha-like experience that people typically associate with it. Sometimes your mind will stay very busy. The difference, however, is that while meditating, you aim to be a non-judgmental witness or observer of whatever you're experiencing and thinking, rather than having your thoughts take over and becoming them. By not making it wrong, and lovingly accepting it, you can then choose the focus you'd prefer, and allow a good-feeling experience to emerge. I'll get into tips and strategies for this in a moment.

With the right strategies and approach, your meditation time can also be very relaxing and a nice change in pace and focus. If your body is needing more rest, you might even fall asleep. I personally think there's more to be gained by being aware when you meditate, though. So, if you want to stay aware and awake, there's less risk of falling asleep if you stay seated. If, however, you could use a good, short power nap, or just want a full-body, letting go, deep relaxation experience, feel free to lie down to meditate. You might sleep, and you might not. And the rest might be a good recharge. This often works for me. I call it a "reboot". and 20-30 minutes is usually perfect.

Sometimes you might visualize. Sometimes you might have thoughts you hear. And, sometimes you might just have a "sense" about something. Your experience can happen through any of your senses and in any way.

You can have emotional experiences, too. When you step into the space of Spirit, you might also experience its love; although not necessarily always in a big, wow way. Just like you love your partners, or your family and friends, even your pets, sometimes you feel it in a big way; but most of the time it's more subtle. *It just is.* And you act from that love, and you know it's there. While meditating, you might feel Spirit's love in these various ways. It's just delicious when this happens.

Spirit is also peace, joy, and *all* good-feeling emotions, especially the feelings of inner peace, calm, stillness, quiet, and love. When you feel any of them, you are experiencing Spirit, and you're experiencing Spirit experiencing through you. There's a whole spectrum of good-feeling emotions and intensities. *When you feel good in any way, notice it. Acknowledge it. "THIS is Spirit feeling through me! This is who I am!"*

It's important to remember that although you can have very special experiences while meditating, it's not that it's *supposed* to happen. Nothing is "supposed" to happen. Meditation is merely a means to practice being mindful – to cultivate your awareness of your thoughts and to develop more choice over what you want to focus on and how you want to be. And, it's an opportunity to experience yourself as your whole Spirit and to nurture this.

In the world of meditation, it's said that there's only one "bad" meditation; and that's not showing up to meditate. If a technique or approach works for you, then it's a good one. If you feel like you can meditate while hanging upside down, then all the power to you! In my opinion, it's okay to move, to scratch, to yawn, to clear your throat or cough if needed, to wipe your nose. If my cat is mewing at the door to go out or to come in, I get up and take care of him while maintaining my relaxed state, and then return to my meditation position and focus. Get the point? I believe it's okay to do what you need to be and stay comfortable. I don't think of meditation as a discipline, like training in the military. I like to think of it as a joy, and a gentle drifting in and out.

In sum, I believe meditation should feel good, and be easy and light, rather than serious and disciplined. And, never mind what you have heard meditation *should* be. That pressure alone will keep you from reaching a deep state! Let go of "I'm not doing this right.", and just let it be whatever it is for you. Whatever happens is okay. The more you practice, the more likely it will be that you'll have pleasant, feeling-good, and maybe even insightful meditation experiences. Like anything, the more you practice, the better it gets.

Some easy meditation tips and strategies

Some basic tips

I've mentioned a few times that having thoughts is a part of meditation; and that the goal is to be a witness to them. When a thought shows up that isn't useful, or is distracting from what you'd like, simply say something like, "I'm just *having* a thought." Or, "There's thinking again." Or, "(your name) is having thoughts." (Tip: When you speak about yourself in the third person, it helps you separate yourself from the thoughts and be more objective.) Then just return to whatever meditation strategy you're using. Remember to just notice your thoughts like cars going by. You don't have to take each one for a ride. You get to choose.

If you're sitting, sit in a way that does not stress any part of your body; so that it's easy to maintain the position without any discomfort or strain; and so that you can easily lose awareness of your body. For example, keep your head upright, rather than letting it hang down, which would strain your neck. Also to prevent any strain, keep your shoulders and back up and evenly balanced, and your feet on the floor. Think of being balanced and aligned, and open to receive. If you desire a grounding experience, you can place your palms down on your thighs. If you prefer an open, receiving experience, play with some form of having your palms up and open. Of course, these are just suggestions, not rules.

How you breathe will also make a difference in how easy it is for you to relax. Try this: Focus on just the upper part of your chest, and take a big breath, trying to fill that space. How does it feel? Relaxing, or more tense? This is a very common way of breathing, and of taking a big, supposedly relaxing breath. However, it actually tends to create more of an anxious feeling for most people. How about you?

Now focus on your lower belly. You can even place your hands there, off to the sides of your belly a bit; so that your fingers are on your belly and your thumbs and palms are more along your sides. Now take a nice, slow, full breath that begins down there and fills and expands that whole area, and continues to move up through your whole chest. You'll feel your whole inner body cavity expand. Breathing through your nose seems to make this deeper breathing a little easier, too.

At the very least, you'll feel your belly rise and fall as you breathe. If you watch a young child breathe, this is what you'll see. It's the natural, healthier way to breathe, and creates a calming effect. Play around with this until you get it, and practice. Nothing forceful. You're going for easy and full and relaxed.

Some spiritual teachings say that your breath is Spirit energy moving through you. Since everything is Spirit energy, this must be so. But thinking of it as Spirit moving through you can be a kinda cool way to experience it. We're just always playing with our imagination anyway, after all.

Okay. You've got yourself in a comfortable position, and you're breathing in a way that is relaxing and expanding. And, you're letting yourself just witness your thoughts without getting caught up in them. You could just continue doing this, and nothing more. Your meditation could be just focusing on your breath, and returning to the focus of your breath when undesirable thoughts show up; just enjoying the simplicity and peace of this relaxing, special time for being your Whole Spirit-Self.

I like having options available to me. Just having one method for meditating gets boring for me. Even when I settle into one that I love, some days it just might not work for me. So it's great to have another approach to play with. Here are some easy meditation strategies you can try.

Some different ways you can easily meditate

There are so many ways to meditate. Here are some of my favorites that I, and the many people I've taught, find the easiest to use.

- I love softly playing meditative music in the background. Music is vibration, and so are we. Find music that feels meditative to you. It might be classical music. It might be New Age. There's an almost infinite selection available for you through the internet radio stations such as Pandora and Jango, and also on YouTube. I like using music with specific frequencies embedded in that help you meditate and tune your body. For example, search on YouTube for Solfeggio frequency meditation music, and try some out. Each day, find one that feels right as you listen to it. Your body will let you know what you're needing that day.
- You can simply enjoy listening to the music with your eyes closed, or you can softly gaze around in appreciation of your surroundings or at something beautiful, like a bouquet of flowers. Or, you can use the music in the background as you use some specific form of meditating. This is my personal preference.

Ideas, with or without music: (Choose one, or play with combining any of them.)

- Just enjoy the simplicity of focusing on the natural, easy rhythms of your breath, breathing fully and slowly from down in your belly, as I explained earlier. Notice the space of expansion and contraction of your breaths. Always begin every meditation with this, as your breath is pivotal to relaxing the mind and body. You can then continue to let this be the focus of your entire meditation or then proceed to another focus, while still maintaining the easy, relaxed breathing.
- Rather than trying to quiet your mind, focus on where the stillness and quiet *already exist* in the space around and within you, in the space of quiet between the sounds, the peace right

there in the midst of whatever, or the quiet and peace in the rhythms of your heart center.

Focusing on any kind of space seems to trigger a relaxation response. Take a moment right now, and notice the quiet that is the space between any sounds in your environment. And, even easier, if you're in a quiet space, focus on that space of quiet and peace. It's always there available to step into. Try my "Space of stillness and quiet" guided meditation to practice this.

- You can spend the time reviewing and *feeling* all that there is to be grateful for – even the simplest of things, like the view out your window, or the sunshine outside, or someone's smile. This will also train your mind to focus on what's good throughout your day. This is a significant strategy for almost effortlessly feeling good during meditation, and throughout your day.

- Imagine or recall a special place that you enjoy, *feel yourself there*, and just hang out there! Or, imagine various representations of states you want to feel, like peace, calm, joy, etc. For example, what image can you bring to mind that makes you feel peaceful and relaxed? Maybe it's a still pond, or a sleeping pet, or gentle waves rolling in and out at the ocean's edge.

- A classic meditation is to move through the parts of your body, deliberately relaxing each part as you go along. You can also imagine that each part can inhale and exhale – releasing tension with each exhale; or imagine someone massaging you, or something similar. Remember to breathe slowly, fully, and to begin down low in your belly. If you like, you can add to this by feeling love and gratitude for each part, even going to your organs, your nervous system, and so on. *Feel appreciation for all that these parts and systems do for you and all that they allow you to experience. Even when a part of us isn't well, there is SO much that IS still healthy and working for you perfectly.*

- You can simply be fully present with your surroundings. Just sit, with eyes softly open, and notice *every single detail* you can see, hear and feel. Think about all that has taken place there. What has this place brought to your life? What are all the things you can appreciate about it? Can you feel Spirit's presence in all that is right there?

- Imagine something you want and *how it will feel* having accomplished or received it – like going on a vacation, or changing a behavior or response. *The feelings are what's most important to focus on, as this is why you want what you want, anyway. How you want to feel is the essence of your desire.* If you want to support a personal change or improve a skill, mentally rehearse it, adjusting it as you go along to be just the way you want to be. Simple as that. Your mind does not know the difference between imagination and reality!

When I was in high school, I did a little downhill skiing with my family. I was very nervous, very slow, and not very good. I was pretty stuck at the snowplow stage.

One night before going skiing the following day, I decided to dream about myself skiing effortlessly, swooshing down the slopes. The next day was a very different, more positive experience, and I was able to do more moves more easily, as well!

I also applied this strategy while in my NLP training. I would set an intention at night to practice my NLP skills while sleeping, in a way that still allowed me to fully get the sleep and rest I needed. As I've mentioned, I ended up excelling in my group, in great part because of the dream practicing that helped develop my ability to let go to an unconscious competence. So, my point is, using your imagination is another easy, pleasing means for creating what you desire!

Back to some more ways you can meditate with ease:

- You can simply say affirmations or mantras to yourself that help you to focus on thoughts that feel good and direct you in ways that you like. For example, I love using words such as "peace" or "love" or "joy" or "thank you". In the guided meditations selection, you'll find one called, "I am here." It's a beautiful mantra that brings you to your presence in the moment, and the presence of Spirit within you, around you, and as you.

- Once you're relaxed in your meditation, you can use it to set intentions for the *essence* of how you want each segment of your day to go, and/or how you want to be, and imagine it going that way. For example: "It's my intention to move through my day with ease and joy and a lightness of being, trusting that all I need will show up for me." You can also use "I am the space for..." and/or "I am willing and open to....." statements, such as "I am the space for more love, laughter, and friends; and I invite that in." or "I am the space for moving through my day with inner peace, love, ease, and joy." I like "I am open and willing to..." and "I am the space for..." statements because they are softer than "I will" or "I intend to". Try them on. Which ones feel better for you?

- In your imagination, create and hang out in an inner sanctuary, a special, peaceful place to relax, contemplate, and connect to Spirit. Invite in a mentor or person who might have wisdom or guidance to offer you on something you are struggling with.

- Connect with your heart or guides or Spirit for guidance, by simply asking questions. Questions invite in answers and solutions very powerfully.

- Use tapping, which will be covered later in the book, with or without words, to create a relaxation response.

How you can easily incorporate meditating into your life

- Any amount of time is better than no time. Even five minutes of connecting is a great start! Increase the amount of time when you feel inclined to do so, and when you have the time to do so.

- If you like structure, you can make it something you just don't not do – like brushing your teeth or taking your vitamins or medication.

- Again, if you do well with structure or planning, make it a new part of a routine you already have, connecting it to habits that already exist. For example, do you like to sit with your morning coffee or tea? Maybe connect it to that. Getting up a little earlier so you have time for a short meditation can be more valuable than lying in bed longer. You can even do it in your car once you're parked, before getting out! My husband used to do it with headphones while on his bus commute to work.

- Use headphones, and use them to meditate for work breaks, either at your desk or in a quiet space like a spare conference room.

- Don't be extreme about it, like trying to meditate every day. Make a plan that *feels doable*, such as meditating for 15 minutes Sunday morning.

- If you already use some kind of day planner system that works for you, add it in where you really think it can happen.

- Consider doing a little meditation in the morning to set your vibrational momentum for the day, so it will flow with more ease and grace. And do a little before bed as a way to release any tensions of the day and to sink into a peaceful sleep.

Most importantly, don't make it a chore. Don't do it because you think you should or you think it will be good for you. Do it because it feels good! It's a joy! And remember how good it makes you feel when you're thinking about doing it again.

Lighten up; be easy on yourself and enjoy this special, sacred time with your Spirit-Self!

This is a good time to take a break from reading, to try one of my guided meditations. I strongly recommend trying this Guided Meditation Sampler, as it will give you a taste of several of the meditation ideas I've mentioned. Eventually, you'll be able to take off on your own, so you can spend as much time as you like with any aspect of each meditation approach.

To listen to the Meditation sampler, go to www.new possibilitiescoaching.com/three-doorways-to-the-soul-book.html

How being mindful of your body is useful

Let's shift back to the value of being mindful, or aware, of what your body is communicating to you in any moment. Remember, your body is the vehicle for Spirit. "I am Spirit, and I have a body." So, how your body feels is another way for Spirit to communicate to you.

I mentioned earlier that your emotions indicate how aligned you're being in any moment with your Spirit-Self perspective. (Am I getting repetitive? Good!) They let you know if you're being only your "small self", or your whole "Spirit-Self". When you experience undesirable emotions, it's the "static" created by not thinking the way your greater Spirit-Self is thinking about something. Since all of your systems are interconnected, or, actually, just one system, it makes sense that your body will respond to your thoughts. *It provides indicators, or guidance, as to who you're being, just like your emotions do, because it responds to your emotions.*

Again, here are some examples of physical indicators available to you:

- Your posture- whether you're upright and aligned, or slumped over in some fashion
- The degree of muscle tension you're experiencing. How comfortable are you feeling? Tight and tense, or relaxed?
- Your facial muscles and expression, especially your brow and jaw. What emotion is being expressed and felt?
- Your breathing. Is it shallow and up high in your chest, or full and relaxed from down in your belly?
- Even your stomach and digestion could be telling you something.

Many times, maybe even most of the time, we don't notice what we're feeling in our bodies; or, even when we do, we don't do anything about it. If a person were in the room calling your name, you wouldn't ignore it. Right? *Well, discomfort in your body is one way that Spirit is calling you; and it's very helpful to pay attention and respond.*

I'm going to say this more than once, and that's okay. I want you to make a commitment to paying attention to and caring about how you feel, both physically and emotionally; and to not settle for anything you don't like. Honor those feelings as communication from your Soul, from God, that you're not being your whole Spirit-Self, and that it's time to take a moment to use one of the strategies you'll be learning in this book. And, it really only takes a moment! The first step to always take is to breathe and center.

What is centering and why is it needed?

When you get into any fearful or anxious way of thinking, it triggers the amygdala in your brain into a "survival mode", reacting as if your life is actually at risk, a life or death type of risk. When this happens, all resources are directed to your physical needs, so you can literally run away from the danger. It's very primitive! You'll feel this fight-or-flight-or-freeze response in your body, such as tense muscles, shallow breathing, and an increase in heart rate. However, if you chronically live in this stressful state as more of your norm, you might be so used to it that you don't even notice the body's response and communication. And, you'll be at the effect of the toll it can take on you, as well.

Additionally, the more resourceful, frontal lobe part of your brain is shut down; and creates a snowball effect that also prevents you from being able to shift your thinking to Spirit's perspective, or any more useful perspective, for that matter.

Rather than there being a real need to physically run from danger, typically, this survival response is triggered by thinking about possible consequences that we don't want. We're thinking, usually out of our awareness, about possible undesirable "What if" scenarios. "What if I don't get this done on time?", "What if I can't...", "What if something bad happens?", or something similar. What's needed is to be able to think clearly and resourcefully, and to "re-Source", or re-connect to Source, from which there is a solution to every problem. To do so, you first need to deactivate the primitive survival response. This is where centering comes in.

When you're centered, your attention is on the here and now; and you feel fully present, calm, and relaxed. You have full awareness of yourself and your surroundings; and you feel balanced and connected to the earth, like a strong tree not easily tipped over. Ideally, we want to move through our day in a centered manner to feel and be our best.

How to Center

Here's the simple, basic centering process: Bring your focus down to your lower belly, into your "hara" – your "center" just below your navel; and make your breathing slow, full, and deep from your belly. It's the same breathing I explained for meditating. Your belly should expand as you inhale, and go in when you exhale. For centering, if it feels calming, breathe in through your nose, and out through your mouth, even letting out a big relaxing sigh, if you feel inclined. Just breathing through only your nose can work, too. Just feel for what creates the best effect for you.

If you're standing, relax your knees. Continue to breathe like this until you feel a calming effect. This simple step will help you to enter an inner state in which you feel aligned, calmer, relaxed, and centered.

Being centered is a fundamental skill for living with greater harmony, happiness, and success, and relaxing the body so you can live more from your whole Spirit-Self, and to reconnect to your whole Spirit-Self when needed. It's also a very useful resource state for when you want to be your best, or for addressing a crisis or any difficult situation. People who practice martial arts often talk about the importance of being centered and calm, even when they are in the middle of intense competition. In fact, they say that "if you give away your center to your opponent, you have already lost the competition."

Becoming centered is essentially the first step to every strategy and skill you need to be your best Self, including meditating and having access to your inner resources and wisdom, and Spirit perspective. It opens up the possibility of you becoming more aware of your thoughts and emotions and shifting them, and thus shifting from lower vibrations to higher, more allowing ones.

No one is centered all the time. There's a dynamic rhythm. You want to develop the skill of being aware of when you're uncentered (off-balance, restricted, in a survival state, tense, shallow breathing), and being able to shift and return to being centered (calm, relaxed, resourceful, and allowing).

There are two aspects of being centered: grounded and flowing. When grounded, like a tree, we root our center to one spot, making ourselves solid and able to hold or "stand our ground" - holding what we are committed to despite any seemingly external force acting against us.

When flowing, we hold our center and also *move* with whatever comes our way; moving from our center.

Both of these can be appropriate and useful strategies depending upon the situation we are in. The following exercises offer a way to apply the experience of being centered in order to respond more resourcefully to all situations. It will help train you to easily access and maintain this state, and to gain an embodied awareness of when you are centered and when you aren't.

Exercise to demonstrate the impact of being uncentered versus centered:

If you can, it's optimal to find someone to help you experience this at some point. It's pretty cool, and they'll get something out of it, as well.

1. Stand up, and fully recall a situation in which it's usually difficult for you to stay calm, centered, and resourceful, as if you're experiencing it again now. An example might be feeling stressed about something at work, or how you often respond to a certain challenging situation.

   Notice how this uncentered state feels in your body. Where are your attention and your breathing? What are your posture and muscular tension like? What kinds of thoughts are you having? Memorize how you feel so you can notice when you are "off-centered" in the future.

   If available, have someone very gently push you on the shoulder to test your stability, and see what happens. If no one is available, perhaps you can imagine it happening, and tune in to how stable you feel, or not.

2. *Center by bringing your focus down low into your "hara" – your "center" just below your navel; and make your breathing slow, full, and deep from*

your belly; and relax your knees. This simple step will help you to enter an inner state in which you feel aligned, calmer, relaxed and centered.

Notice what this feels like in your body, and memorize it.

3. When you are ready, ask your partner to gently push and pull you in different directions, from different angles (from shoulders, waist, front, back, side to side, etc.), while you practice staying centered, balanced, and aligned both physically and internally.

   As you become more comfortable and confident with your ability to remain centered, you can make it more challenging by asking your partner to push and pull a little harder. You can even experiment with having your partner say things that might normally set you off-center.

4. When you feel ready, hold the centered state and think about the original challenging situation, and notice how your experience is different. How do you feel about the situation now? What kind of thoughts show up now? You should feel much more able to deal with the situation in a resourceful manner.

How you can use centering to shift your state

First, it's important to know the difference between questions and thoughts that limit, versus questions and thoughts that generate desired possibilities.

When we're off-centered, it's very likely that we're having thoughts or asking questions that come from a mood of confusion: "I don't know what's going on, and I don't like it." Examples of confused thoughts might be: "This sucks." "I hate when this happens/ when they do that, etc." "It's not possible."

Often, confused thoughts come in the form of questions like: "Why does this always happen to me?" "Why did this happen to me?" "What did I do wrong?" "Why do I even have to do this?"

Remember how I mentioned earlier that when you ask questions, your mind can't help but search for answers? When you ask yourself these kinds of questions, where does your mind go? Does it start generating answers that open up something new or direct you towards solutions? Not likely. They keep you focused on the problem, and limit, and maybe even close off what's possible for you.

On the other hand, generative questions and thoughts come from a state of perplexity and wonder. These open up a possibility for something positive or new.

Examples could be:

- What questions do I have?
- I wonder....,
- How can this be better?
- What can I learn from this?
- What do I need to function better?
- What's most important right now?
- Who can I ask for help?
- How else could I think about this? What would I say to a good friend about this? How might a role model of mine think about this?
- What else is possible?
- Ask your heart – what would be a more effective response to this?
- Who am I being?
- What's my role in this?
- How CAN I...?
- What IS possible?

- What's the gift/opportunity in this? How could this be happening FOR me?

When you want to shift from a limited way of thinking that doesn't feel good and doesn't open possibilities for you, begin by centering to calm your current response, and then begin opening to something new with generative questions. Here are the steps.

Take a "breather" centering practice:

- Notice when you're in a stressful state. Alternatively, as practice, you can recreate one.
- Breathe from down in your belly, focusing on your "center", just below your navel, and purposefully relax and center by focusing on your belly breathing.
- Next, if you like, you can also expand your awareness into the space of Spirit, by shifting your focus as you did in the Space of Stillness and Quiet meditation. Feel yourself expand into your Wholeness.
- Ask: "How do I want to feel?", and/or "Who am I being?", and/or "Who am I?" (small self or Spirit?)
- "What generative questions can I ask to help me relax further, and to help open up possibilities for what I desire?"

How you can get better at embodying this valuable skill

The more you practice this, the better! One way to accomplish this is to stop and center at least once an hour. At the least, I recommend you make sure you center at least twice a day to build the practice. It takes only as long as a few breaths take, which you'd be taking anyway! How simple can it get?

Ideally, with increased awareness of when you're off-centered, you'll recenter whenever needed. This is what you're aiming for.

Shifting your body to shift your mind

We have the capacity to almost instantly shift our emotional states, it's just that we tend to ruminate in our thoughts and thus maintain the emotions that are in response to them. Good if desirable, not so good if undesirable. We've all seen children shift quickly like this, right?

Here are some other options you can do that make it almost impossible to hold a negative thought. Have some fun actually trying them so you can feel the easy and delightful difference they can make. *As you try each one, try to have a negative thought while holding the posture.*

- Hold prayer hands to your chest/heart area with your head down a bit, sort of in "reverence". (You do not have to have any religion attached to this.)
- Smile, or even just slightly turn the corners of your mouth up, or even just bite down on a pen.
- Shift your posture upright, shoulders back, head up
- Stand with outstretched arms out to sides, with head looking up
- Move – walk, dance, twirl, whatever! The faster, the better.

Adding connecting to Spirit to the centering process, to "Re-Source"

Before you do any more reading in the book, please give yourself about 20 minutes to follow along with the guided "Box into Spirit and Re-Sourcing" meditation. This will help raise your awareness of how you feel when you're being only your smaller physical self or your expanded greater Spirit-Self, and will give you practice with centering and then connecting to Spirit to shift from "s" to "S". From there, you'll notice how much easier it is to be open to your Spirit perspectives, which we will be covering next.

In the meditation, I will be guiding you into feeling the fullness of Spirit and developing a way to quickly re-access it.

Then, I'll have you actually stand and take a few steps forward and fully recall a problematic issue for you. This could be a situation in which you tend to react in undesirable ways. Or, it could be something you tend to worry or stress about. Or, maybe you have "trouble" with someone, and would like to be more resourceful with them. Anything will do in which you typically respond more like your "small self".

Actually standing as I instruct, and using your whole body in this way, is the most powerful way to do this process; but you can experiment with only doing it in your imagination, as well.

After fully re-experiencing your problem issue, we'll leave it in that spot. Then, I'll guide you to step back and return to your Spirit space, and to fully re-access yourself as Spirit/Source again (to "Re-Source"). From there, you'll bring your whole Spirit-Self forward into the problem space, and notice how it changes.

The actual process is easier than it may have just sounded, and I'll be guiding you through each step with ease. It all plays out quite beautifully, and is pretty cool! So, I encourage you to try it. With practice, you'll then be able to apply "Re-Sourcing" in real life. You can imagine how helpful this could be.

To listen to the "Box into Spirit and Re-Sourcing" guided meditation, go to www.newpossibilitiescoaching.com/three-doorways-to-the-soul-book.html

Recap

- Your body is the vehicle for Spirit to create, experience, and expand through you, as you.
- Your body responds to your thoughts.
- Your Soul (Spirit) communicates to you through the doorway of your body through your sensations of comfort and discomfort.

- When your thoughts are aligned with your greater Spirit perspective, you'll feel comfort and ease in your body. When they are not aligned, you'll feel discomfort, or "dis-ease". Thus, it's helpful to be mindful of how you're feeling, and thus who you're being, throughout your day.
- Meditating is a way of practicing mindfulness of your thinking and who you're being, and an easy, relaxing, delicious way of tuning your physical instrument, and your state of mind. It's a spiritual tune-up.
- Centering is a strategy that makes it much easier to be your best, and when stressed, to return to ease and your Spirit-Self's perspectives.
- Both centering and meditating are doorways for returning to Spirit.

We're beginning to build your awareness of how differently it feels when you're being your small self, vs. your greater Spirit Self, and beginning to learn how to shift when needed. Later in the book, we'll also be adding in new narratives and strategies to help with this, too.

For the next week, I invite you to set your intention to notice when your body is letting you know that you're off-centered and being only your "small" self, trying to do and figure it all out from that limited perspective. When that happens, or even if you notice it in some other way- like just feeling bad, take a nice, centering breath from down in your belly (your hara/second chakra), expanding your awareness into the unlimited space of stillness, quiet, peace and Spirit all around and through you. If you like, when you notice being off-centered and small, you can ask yourself, "Who am I being?", then take the expanding breath and say, "I am (your name), and SO much more."

Ideally, with increased awareness of when you're off-centered, you'll re-center whenever needed. Since you're a beginner, at the least, I recommend you make sure you center at least twice a day to build the practice. It takes only as long as a few breaths take, which you'd be taking anyway!

Also, practice being and returning to Spirit by playing with different ways of meditating. *Create a <u>doable</u> goal for yourself, like once or twice this week for 5- 10 minutes.* It's nice to have a variety of ways at your disposal. Some days, one way of meditating may not work, even though it's one of your favorites. If so, just move into another strategy. You might enjoy the variety, as well.

CHAPTER FOUR

Holding the Perspective of Spirit Consciousness

"The Soul is not a thing. It is a place from which we speak."

Julio Ollala

First, let me define for you what I'm meaning in this book when I talk about the perspective you and Spirit are holding. Simply put, I'm referring to how you're thinking about something, and thus, who you're being – your small self, or your Spirit-Self. It's your language doorway to your Soul.

I've presented the idea that your Soul, or Spirit, is always guiding you and communicating to you through your emotions and body. When they feel good, it's guidance that your thoughts, or how you're languaging your experience and talking to yourself, are aligned with the perspective of Spirit Consciousness. You're being your greater Self. And, when they don't feel good, it's a red flag alerting you that your thoughts are not the perspective that Spirit is holding on the same topic, and you're being your smaller self.

"The quantum field responds not to what you want, it responds to who you are being."

Dr. Joe Dispenza

When you are not holding the point of view of Spirit on a particular topic, even though you *are* always Spirit, you are only *experiencing* life at that time as a smaller version of yourself. This version is much more limited, less likely to manifest desires, and usually experiences less inner peace, joy, and ease. Life tends to be harder when you don't use all the resources and powers available as your Whole Self. It's like not using your household's electricity. Using the power of your household electricity sure makes life easier, right? Why not plug into the power of Source Energy?!

Another term I'll be using is "presupposition". A presupposition is what we presuppose, or assume, or hold as true. *It's not necessarily "the" truth, but we hold it as such.* So, a presupposition is a perspective, a way of thinking. To keep things simple, I use the two words pretty interchangeably. When I ask, "What would the perspective of Spirit be around this concern?", I'm asking, "What would Spirit hold as true about this concern?"

When we presuppose that we are Spirit, we will think about things differently than when we think of ourselves as only a physical human being, separate from Spirit, and nothing more.

In other words, when we presuppose we are all one with Spirit, all unified in the Field of Infinite Potential, the usefulness of all our presuppositions as a *separate* self comes into question and they change. In this section of the book, I'm going to share with you a list of presuppositions from the perspective of Spirit that I have found to be more useful, and very powerful, compared to the presuppositions that stem from believing you are not Spirit. Again, it's my claim that no one really knows *the* truth. Thus, I am not claiming they are the truth. I'm claiming they are useful when *held* as true. I invite you to try them out and see if they are useful for you. Of key importance, I believe, is coming to see for yourself that we humans are already and always presupposing something.

So, what does Spirit Consciousness, the greater part of who you are, hold as true? This list I'm providing is not all-inclusive, of course;

but I believe, and have found in my work, that these are the primary, essential ones that can have a significant impact and will serve you well. Feel free to add more! They come from what I've collected and used from many spiritual teachers, such as Esther Hicks who channels Abraham (collective Spirit consciousness), Wayne Dyer, Deepak Chopra, Michael Beckwith, Sonia Miller, Elizabeth Purvis, Allison Phillips, Mike Dooley, Bruce Lipton, Eckhart Tolle, Dr. Joe Dispenza, and more.

As Spirit, you presuppose: "I am Spirit, and I have a body."

I addressed this earlier, in the levels of consciousness. This is very significant for remembering who you are and what you're capable of. As Spirit, my thoughts are like, "I am Ann Ide, and SO much more. I am Spirit, here to create, express, expand and experience through and as this unique human masterpiece. I (Spirit) am here to experience this very temporary human experience of Ann Ide. The part of me that is Source Energy is the greater part of who I am. My human experience is minuscule by comparison."

As Spirit, the energetic part of you, or your Soul, is eternal; and you have available to you all that Spirit is and is capable of. All the love, wisdom, inner peace, ease, and creative powers.

How does that feel? If you believe it, it will feel amazing! If not, you won't; and, I believe that feeling comes from not matching the belief that Spirit holds as true.

An opposing belief would be something like, "All I am is my physical body and mind." When you hold this as true, what limitations show up? How does it feel? Really feel this before continuing.

Are there times when you forget your Spirit-Self perspective and slip into this instead, like when you get injured or sick, or when you feel like you have too much to do? Recall how that feels when it happens.

Remember how that emotional guidance from Spirit feels, reminding you that you are not perceiving the situation from your Spirit-Self perspective.

And when those undesirable feelings show up of being merely physical, or limited or small in some way, let those feelings remind you to take a big, relaxing, centering breath, and to return to "I am (your name), and SO much more! I am Spirit!" It will feel so much better, and open up new possibilities for you!

I am a creator

Why do we sometimes call Spirit "Source Energy"? Because Spirit is the source of the energy of all that is. It's also the creative source, or creator, of all that is. If you are an extension of Source (the wave in the ocean), then you must also be a creator. When you have thoughts, you are creating, whether it's what you want, or what you don't want! And, it means that when you have a desire, you are creating! What a power to own and to learn how to use effectively!

How does that feel? Do you like it?

An opposite belief or perspective would be something like: "There is no Spirit or anything non-physical that's creating, and certainly not me. Reality is what I see, and that's all there is, and that's what I get. It happens. I can do my best with my mind and body to manage circumstances and achieve what I want by making things happen through my actions."

How does that feel? For me, it feels like I'm greatly at the effect of my circumstances; and it feels like hard work is inevitable. It also feels like there are fewer possibilities. Have there been times when you've slipped into this way of thinking, forgetting that you're a creator? Of course! What are some examples for you? How did you feel?

Remember how that emotional guidance from Spirit felt, reminding you that you were not perceiving the situation from your Spirit-Self perspective.

When it happens again, let how you feel be your reminder from Spirit to take a big, relaxing, centering breath, and to return to, "I am an extension of Spirit, and I am a creator! I can create what I want!"

Unlimited abundance and possibilities for accomplishing my desired outcomes are available to me.

Since you exist in and create from a field of pure potentiality and infinite possibilities, of course unlimited abundance and possibilities are available to you!

What you create will merely depend on your thoughts, focus and attention, beliefs, and your alignment with your Source Self perspective. By holding Source perspective, you are tuning in to the frequency of Spirit, and, to use our earlier analogy, the radio station playing what you desire.

How does this feel when you try it on? Freeing, perhaps? What else shows up for you?

A non-Spirit perspective might be something like, "My possibilities are limited. The only way to create is by physically manipulating what already exists in "reality".

How does that feel? Really feel this before continuing.

Recall a time when you've felt this way. Which perspective feels better and opens up more for you?

The next time you feel limited in your possibilities, let those restricted feelings be your reminder from Spirit to take a big, relaxing, centering breath, and to return to, *"I exist in and create from a field of pure potentiality and infinite possibilities, therefore unlimited abundance and possibilities are available to me!*

Uncertainty means unlimited possibilities are still available.

Usually, when we want certainty, we're focused on things working out the way we want in one particular way that we have in mind. At best, we might have a few options. The main point is that we're focused on *what we've already thought of.*

However, the previous presupposition reminds us that *unlimited* possibilities for accomplishing your desired outcomes are available to you. *The Universe can orchestrate what you desire in ways that may not even occur to you.*

By embracing uncertainty, allowing more than one option/possibility, and letting go of attachment to *if* and *how* your desires are fulfilled, you become open to allowing the field of all possibilities and intelligence to do its work in possibly unimaginable ways. When you are detached in this way, you will experience all the fun, adventure, magic, and mystery of life.

In one of our Doorways to the Soul programs, there was a woman who had been out of work for close to a year, and she was the main breadwinner for her family of 5. She had been looking and looking for more work that fit into what she thought she would qualify for and would be right for her, and nothing was happening. She was quite anxious and worried.

As we were covering these presuppositions, she had a big "Aha moment". "You mean other things are possible that I haven't thought of? There are unlimited possibilities for me?!!" She let go of her knowing how it had to go. Within a few weeks, a colleague she used to work with called her from his new job. He said there was a director position open that she would be perfect for, and encouraged her to apply. Previously, she didn't think she was director material. She went for it, and got the position, with even more than she would have asked for (flex time, remote work options, etc.) Tada!

How does it feel to presuppose this new definition of uncertainty; that it can now mean *unlimited possibilities are still available to you?* Doesn't this open up so much more than having *only one* possibility available? I think it presents much better odds of things working out for you. If the idea that things are uncertain used to provoke fear and anxiety, then perhaps now you'll be able to stay open with eager anticipation of the intelligence of the Universe working in magical ways for you.

A non-Spirit perspective might be something like, "I'm certain that there are a limited number of ways that things can turn out the way I want. I need to know. I won't be happy/okay, etc. unless this happens the way I want it; and I know I'm right."

How does that feel? Really feel this before continuing.

Recall a time when you've felt something similar to this. Remember how that emotional guidance from Spirit felt, reminding you that you were not perceiving the situation from your Spirit-Self perspective.

Which perspective feels better and opens up more ways for things to work out for you? Which feels safer now?

The next time you feel anxious about things being uncertain, let those fearful feelings be your reminder from Spirit to take a big, relaxing, centering breath, and to return to, "Uncertainty means unlimited possibilities are still available for me!"

I can be, do, or have anything I desire. And, I have all I need within me to be the creator of and have the solutions for all I desire.

Since Spirit is all-knowing and all-creative power, and you are an extension, and a part of this field of infinite intelligence, all of the answers and solutions you seek are available to you when you are tuned into it.

According to spiritual teachings, there are laws of the Universe. One of them is the law of deliberate creation. The essence of it is that you create as you speak and think, both consciously and unconsciously. Your creative power is in your thinking. In the next part of the book, we'll be getting into how to use this power most effectively. For now, just know that as Spirit, you have all the powers of Spirit available to you! You only have to learn how to use them.

Assuming you *will* learn how to use your innate power to create and to receive the solutions you need, how does presupposing this feel? In my experience, it's like being a magician or wizard; and so much fun! As with all of these presuppositions, fears fall away when you really remember to perceive through your Spirit-Self.

When we forget who we really are, we tend to unconsciously live from the belief that only certain things are possible; and therefore, because our thoughts create, that becomes true. However, there are infinite possibilities, even if you're not aware of what they may be. Of course, this includes lack. As the author Richard Bach said, "Argue for your limitations and they are yours, as well."

When you are perceiving as only your smaller self, you might think something like, "Just because I can imagine it, doesn't mean I can be, do or have it. I may not be enough for what I want. (or some other reason.) Only some things are possible."

How does this feel? Really feel this before continuing.

Recall a time when you felt like something you wanted wasn't possible. I bet there have been a lot of these times! Remember how that emotional guidance from Spirit felt, reminding you that you were not perceiving the situation from your Spirit-Self perspective.

The next time you feel like something you want isn't possible, let those doubtful feelings be your reminder from Spirit to take a big, relaxing, centering breath, and to return to, "I am an extension of Spirit, with all of its powers and wisdom available to me. I create as I speak and think; and as I tune into the field of infinite intelligence, all the answers and solutions I need are also available to me."

I am responsible for my experience. Everything I experience is a reflection of my vibration, thoughts, and focus.

According to the law of attraction, "like attracts like", meaning, you will experience what you focus on and/or think about, and thus, what you become a matching vibration for, whether you're aware of it, or not. Using our radio analogy again, you will only hear the station that you are tuned into.

Notice that it says you are responsible for your "experience". Of course, you're not responsible for everything that happens in the world, and you cannot control all of life. There are dynamics outside of us. Neither you nor I created the Covid-19 Corona virus pandemic. However, how you respond to outer circumstances and how you manage your thoughts, focus, and vibration, will determine how you are affected by them. Ever wonder why some people have more "bad luck" or drama in their life than others? Ever wonder why not everyone is affected in the same way by the same experience? It's not just luck.

Sometimes Spirit wants a certain experience with the intention of growth and expansion for you, or perhaps others. Its intelligence might be at play in ways we cannot see or understand. We just can't always know all the dynamics at play. However, if you ask yourself, "How can this be happening FOR me, rather than to me? What opportunities or gifts might come out of this?", you open yourself to something positive in the experience, and experiencing it with greater ease.

This presupposition does not mean you should go blaming yourself or feeling guilty when things go "wrong". We are not ever going to be "perfect" beings. We can, however, accept experiences as feedback and opportunities for learning, and getting better and better. Rather than berating yourself and thinking, "How did I do this to myself?", you can ask the same question with open curiosity, or even wonder, eager to uncover an opportunity for improvement. When you do this, it DOES get better and better!

From this perspective, you are never a victim. Rather than being at the effect of anything or anyone outside of you, your experience depends on YOU. How empowering is that?! Maybe now you can realize that you have more control than you've ever thought before.

My husband, Mark, and I always say, with full belief, "Everything always works out for us." And, you know what? One way or another, that's what happens! Remember, as an extension of Spirit, you are all that Spirit is and has. Accept and embrace your creative powers, rather than accepting that you can be a victim to circumstances.

So, how does that feel? If it seems a little scary to accept such responsibility, keep in mind that as you learn and practice more of the strategies in this book, your level of competence will improve. As that happens, you'll feel good about being in charge of your own experience.

In contrast, when you are perceiving experiences as only your smaller self, you might think something like, "There is only one, fixed reality, and it's what I see/experience. I have little control over it, can't change it, it's all fate, etc.; and my thoughts don't matter/have little power."

How does this feel? Really feel this before continuing.

Recall a time when you felt fearful about how something at work, or in the world, or even just in traffic might affect you. Remember how that emotional guidance from Spirit felt, reminding you that you were not perceiving the situation from your Spirit-Self perspective.

The next time you feel like you don't have control or are at the effect of your circumstances, or are afraid of something "bad" happening, *let those anxious feelings be your reminder from Spirit to take a big, relaxing, centering breath, and to return to, "I am responsible for my experience. Everything I experience is a reflection of my vibration, thoughts, and focus." Then you can shift to one of these Spirit perspectives that feels most appropriate. (An exercise for practicing this is provided.)*

"Ask and you shall receive." Inherent within every intention and desire are the mechanics for their fulfillment.

When you have a desire, the way for *the essence* of your desire (*why* you want something) to manifest in *physical* form exists in *non-physical* form, in what we call the field of potential.

From your desire, the infinite, organizing power of the Universe goes to work for you, and then, *"It is done!"* It will exist as a vibrational frequency, or a vibrational reality, that will manifest in a physical form available to your senses when you tune in to the frequency of that vibrational reality. You are the radio tuner, deciding what you get to hear by deciding what you're going to tune into. The more you think as your greater Spirit-Self, the more tuned in you will be to the field where your desire is "playing" for you (like the song playing on the radio station you're tuned into).

A wonderful analogy for this concept of "It is done" is when you place an order for something, either online or on the phone. Once you've placed the order, you know for sure that you'll be receiving it. It's done! That same feeling of knowing and certainty is the vibration that will bring your desires to you. Spirit knows it is done; and now you can, too.

I've also been playing with the concept of "Siri" or "Alexa", when we simply ask, or say what we want, like, "Alexa, play the song I wanna hold your hand." It's a simple request-and-receive process that we're starting to take for granted. We can presume the same when we ask Spirit, or "the Universe" for something!

How to ask effectively

This doesn't mean that what you ask for is necessarily done *specifically* the way you imagine it. However, the essence of the desire, or why you want it, is done. Let's say you want more money. Money is the "specific" I'm referring to. Why do you want more money? For the freedom to travel? To live someplace that's an upgrade for you? For the feeling of freedom to do and have what you desire? Those things are the essence – the "why" you want more money. Focus on that, and feel what it will be like.

You also don't need to focus on *how* it will be delivered. Again, you only need to focus on what it will feel like to actually experience the essence of your desire manifested, and, have no conflicting beliefs. We'll get more into the aspect of beliefs later.

If you start trying to figure out only from your small self how to get more money, you'll very likely get yourself in an overwhelming tizzy, challenging all your beliefs about how it could be possible for you. Let that go, and allow the inspired ideas and surprising means to show up for you. Here's an example.

Years ago, our family of four was living in a small 4 room apartment, and I was driving our kids back and forth to their alternative private school 30 minutes each way every day. I had been wanting, and thus asking for, a bigger home for us. I didn't know how it would be possible, as it seemed that all of our money was going into the school tuition. But I kept imagining how it would feel, and trusted it would unfold somehow. One day, I felt inspired to just check an online realty site for what was available and what prices were like around the school. There at the top of the page, was my dream home, 3 minutes from the kids' school; and it had been available for over a year already! It was everything I had been asking for. All it needed was a bunch of painting. And, because it had been vacant so long, we were able to negotiate the price down. But wait, there's more to this beautiful story.

This home was still going to cost us almost $1000 more per month than we were accustomed to; and our income was a fixed, salaried income at the time. Nevertheless, we took the leap, trusting that somehow it would work out for us! Two weeks after moving there, Mark was laid off due to a company reorganization.

Now, most people would react to that news with something like, "Oh, no!" Was that your automatic reaction when you read what happened to us?

We didn't. Having been through this before, and already practicing a more Spiritual perspective, rather than freaking out, we just declared it as an opportunity for something better. Eventually, that's what happened, enabling us to pay for our increased expenses!

Once you've asked, and you're trusting in the Universe orchestrating it and providing it for you; part of that orchestrating might be you receiving thoughts and ideas that inspire you to take some kind of action towards what you want. When these ideas come from you being your Whole Self, they are usually right on target and flow with ease. If, however, you're taking action from your smaller self, thinking out of fear and the need to control things from a merely physical approach, it may take effort and won't feel as joyful.

In the same vein, you also want to be asking from a space of Spirit perspective, knowing that abundance is a given, that all you desire is possible, and so on. When you ask from your smaller-self perspective, from a sense of fear, lack, or control, your focus is then on what you *don't* want, and thus will only perpetuate that.

The way to sense which perspective you're asking from is by noticing your mood. This will be your emotional guidance, or feedback, as to how aligned you are with your Spirit-Self perspective, and what your vibration is. As mentioned before, it will indicate if you're tuning into the frequency of the "radio station" of the preferred reality of your fulfilled desire.

For example, asking for more money from your small-self perspective and lack might sound like this, "I need more money because I don't have enough for.... or because I don't have what I want." Asking from your Spirit-Self might sound like, "I love and appreciate what I have; and it would be so nice to also have...., or, I'd love to be able to say "YES!" to whatever I like! That would be so much fun! It's done! Thank you, thank you!"

Remember, it's not just the words you use. What matters is what you're holding as true as you speak them and the mood and vibration that will create for you. If you're saying one thing, but believing another, the belief will predominate. As we continue through the book, you'll learn ways to deal with inner conflicts like this. Pay particular attention to the section on "Tips for how to talk about what you want and telling your new believable story."

Start playing with all of this with baby steps, asking for things that you can believe in manifesting for you. Then, the more you experience how beautifully this works, the more you'll be able to trust and expect it for anything.

It can be such fun! Can you feel that possibility? It's how all the eager anticipation of Christmas can feel like as a kid.

In contrast, when you are perceiving experiences as only your smaller self, you might think something like, "My desires might be fulfilled, and might not. It's up to me to make it happen by manipulating my external, material world."

How does this feel? Really feel this before continuing.

Recall a time when you felt doubt or fear about whether something you wanted would manifest for you. Remember how that emotional guidance from Spirit felt, reminding you that you were not perceiving the situation from your Spirit-Self perspective.

The next time you feel that kind of doubt or fear, let those feelings be your reminder from Spirit to take a big, relaxing, centering breath, and to return to, "When I ask, it is done!"

I allow others their experience because as Source/Spirit, there is no right or wrong.

Spirit is all-loving and all-accepting, and does not judge anything or anyone as "right" or "wrong". Humans, however, with the free wills and minds we have been given, create right and wrong by the interpretations and meanings we attach to people and their actions. We have been given the free will to choose for ourselves how we want to perceive things. The question is, is your perception serving you? How does it make you feel?

ALL people are extensions of Spirit. Spirit has intentionally manifest as each of us, to have unique experiences. How can we judge Spirit for wanting those experiences as right or wrong?

Additionally, even though it may not be apparent from our human perspective, on a Spiritual level, every person is learning about their connection to The Universe and its power, too. We are all learning and evolving a new understanding of who we really are, Source Energy at play. And, where a person is at on this huge spectrum, will show up differently for everyone.

Through their thoughts, focus, and attention, like you, *everyone* is a creator of their reality. And, *each person's reality is valid to them.* Just like yours feels valid to you. From Source's perspective, there is no one truth, no one right way. It is an all-inclusive Universe.

When you let go of making people right or wrong in their choices, and see them as Spirit sees them, and remember that they are Spirit at play, you'll experience less impatience and anger, and you'll experience more inner and outer love and peace.

Now, since we have free will, we will often have different preferences and standards than others; and there might be contexts in which you need others to have similar preferences as yours, like in partnerships, in work, and with those you live with. Without making anyone "wrong", you can work on finding ways to make it work despite differences, or find compromises, or choose to go separate ways.

Additionally, as humans, we can form some useful agreements about right and wrong behaviors, like which side of the road to drive on, and not harming others.

There's an indigenous tribe that has a beautiful way of dealing with people who break their rules for what's right. When someone does this, they hold a ritual in which the community surrounds the rule-breaker in a circle, ceremoniously showering them with love to help return them to their Whole Self, who would never do harm. They still see the person from a loving perspective.

Imagine lovingly and peacefully accepting people as Spirit manifest as who they uniquely are, and where they're at, and working things out from that space. How might that go differently than it does for you now? How might it feel?

In contrast, when you are perceiving people as only your smaller self, you might think something like, "There's a right and wrong way to be/do, and I know what it is. I resent others for being wrong."

How does this feel? Really feel this before continuing.

Recall a time when you felt impatient, angry, or resentful towards someone. Remember how that emotional guidance from Spirit felt, reminding you that you were not perceiving the situation from your Spirit-Self perspective.

The next time you feel that kind of impatience, anger, or judgment of someone, let those feelings be your reminder from Spirit to take a big, relaxing, centering breath, and to return to, "I allow others their experience because each person is Spirit manifest and at play; and, as Source/Spirit, there is no right or wrong. It's an all-inclusive Universe."

Contrast (what you don't want), diversity, and polarities are all part of the process of creation and growth, and evolution, personally and collectively. Therefore, I can accept and even appreciate all of it. All is well from this perspective.

Remember the universal cycles of change? In that cycle, turbulence and chaos are part of the cycle of growth and change. There is evidence of this in all systems. As I mentioned before, when we maintain and act from this awareness, we can feel more at ease about what's going on, and take actions, and make decisions accordingly.

Additionally, we must have the awareness of what we don't like or want to know what we do want. Same with opposites, or polarities. We could not know empty if we did not know full. It's just how it works!

From these contrasting experiences, desires are born, and something new is created (done!).

When a woman goes into labor to give birth, we don't say something is wrong or feel bad about it. Someone is being born! In fact, the more a woman relaxes into the birthing pains, the less pain she tends to experience and the easier the birth can be. It's definitely an accepting and allowing process.

Life is a process of birthing one desire after another, and we came here to enjoy the whole process from the birthing of the desire through the unfolding of its manifestation. It's a beautiful thing!

How does it feel when you hold this perspective? Can you relax into it?

In contrast, when you are perceiving life as only your smaller self, you might think something like, "Anything that doesn't feel good is bad, something's wrong."

How does this feel? Really feel this before continuing.

Recall a time when you felt bad or anxious about how things were going. Remember how that emotional guidance from Spirit felt, reminding you that you were not perceiving the situation from your Spirit-Self perspective.

The next time you experience something like this, when you aren't appreciating the value of the contrast, let those feelings be your reminder from Spirit to take a big, relaxing, centering breath, and to return to, "New desires and creation are being born from this contrast, and it's my intention to allow their manifestation."

There is only a Source of well-being, and I either allow it in or not.

All of my spiritual learning has confirmed for me that there are no evil spirits; nor does Spirit ever punish or "teach you a lesson". Spirit is ever-ready to shower us with all the love and good that we desire. What we actually manifest from the field of pure potential is dependent on us, on what we focus on, and our vibrational frequency. This is pretty much the same as the presupposition, "Everything I experience is a reflection of my vibration and focus." YOU are the creator.

This presupposition usually brings up some doubts and questions for people. So, let me address the main question that shows up.

What about all the pain and suffering in the world?

If you only consider *from your physical, human perspective* that there is only a Source of pure, positive well-being, you'll probably have difficulty wrapping your thoughts and emotions around it. From our human perspective, this certainly doesn't seem to be true.

However, what we're exploring here, and what I'm inviting you to try, is what *Spirit's* perspective is. Additionally, as I mentioned earlier, I'm not claiming any of this to be *the* truth, necessarily; even though many spiritual teachers will say otherwise. I'm suggesting that these presuppositions can be useful, and have been for me.

Much of life, and how the divine intelligence of Spirit works, is a mystery beyond what most of us are able to comprehend. We want it all to be simple rather than complex and mysterious. We want certainty and control rather than being open to the unknown. However, those desires are human, survival-based desires, from conditioned programming we're being called to grow beyond.

Here are some of my thoughts on what *Spirit's* perspective might be on what we tend to think of as the pain and suffering in the world.

Everything that happens in life just is. There's no good or bad, or otherwise. It's neutral. Anything other than that is experienced through the meaning we each place on it, or the assessments and interpretations we create about it. Hence, the same circumstance can be experienced differently by different people (more on this in chapter 5). It's possible that what you perceive as someone else's suffering is not being experienced exactly as you imagine it. I'm not saying this is a singular explanation or possibility, only that it could be one possible factor for some situations.

I remember when we lived in our small apartment, and some people would say things like, "How can you do that?", implying that it must be so hard and difficult. But that wasn't our experience at all! Similarly, there are people in the world living with much less and in very different conditions than we're accustomed to; and we might tend to think that they suffer because of it. That's not always the case, though. Many of them are very joyful people! That's what they know, and they most likely look at things differently than we do. So, that's one possible factor to consider.

Very significant for me, is the point that Spirit is eternal, all-creative power. Our bodies die, but the greater part of who we are continues on in transcendent love, peace, ease, and joy. Each physical experience is a very temporary manifestation and experience Spirit is having for the sake of having the experience, and for further growth and evolution. Each physical experience is merely Spirit at play, like when you played pretend as a child. You played with no attachment to the experience as if it were real. You knew it was pretending and temporary.

Or, how about when you watch a horror or sad movie? You willingly feel all the emotions of it with pleasure! Why? Because you know it's not real, and only temporary.

These are examples of what I imagine Spirit's perspective is of everything that happens here on planet Earth (and elsewhere). Remember, "I am Spirit, and I have a body." I know it can be rather challenging to grasp the idea that our human experiences aren't actually "real"; because the design is for us to experience them as real! It wouldn't be much of a game of pretend if it didn't feel real, would it?

I also believe that Spirit comes through as each of us with a unique, divine plan, or purpose, which can be fulfilled in an infinite number of ways. Sometimes that plan might be in service to some greater good, like for the transformation of another person, or for greater evolution and change. It might be a divine orchestration beyond what we, in our human mindset, can see or understand, or even accept.

Let's also consider the universal cycles of change and the roles of turbulence and chaos. If you think about it historically, most struggle, tragedy, and suffering have eventually been a stimulus or at least a part of the process towards change and evolution. It usually doesn't happen as easily and quickly as we'd like. Sometimes, from our human perspective, it even seems like progress isn't happening at all. But imagine the perspective of being eternal (which the greater part of you actually is). What we perceive as a long time (even centuries, as an example), is probably the teeniest, tiniest, beyond words that we have for how small a blip in time it is.

I believe life now is actually better than it was in the past; and that, even though sometimes we even temporarily regress, change has and is happening for the better. I would not want to be living at any other time in history.

Sometimes I wonder if when people die in great numbers, like in pandemics or wars, that it's nature's way of letting go and reorganizing in some fashion (another cycle of growth). It happens with other aspects of nature and wildlife all the time. Why do we think it couldn't happen with humans, as well? Just a thought.

Then there's the factor called the law of attraction. It's at work whether we're aware of it, or not. If that's so, then wouldn't the focus and vibration of individuals and of a collective group of people influence what their experience is?

When Donald Trump was up for election as president, there was a very large collective consciousness focused on their fears if he were elected, and on what they didn't want (for him to be elected). Remember, when you focus on what you *don't* want, according to the law of attraction, you'll get what you're focused on- what you *don't* want. There apparently was also a large collective consciousness on desiring him to be president. I believe his getting elected was a perfect example of the law of attraction at work. We got what we were focused on.

Here's something else I've heard and really resonates with me. Everything that is occurring is happening with a higher purpose in mind. The ultimate outcome is more love and compassion, and the increased awareness and unfolding of who we truly are. All souls involved in all situations and events knew what they were going to participate in.

When you see the circumstances and events from the grander perspective that Source has, you know that everyone is going to be okay. You know that we are all eternal. You know who we all truly are. You know that everyone will eventually remember this and return to this, and be okay. And you know that *everything* is occurring for the remembrance of "love is all there is"; and *everything* is occurring for you/us to become more of who you/we truly are.

Take a big breath, and let the beauty of that sink in. Maybe even re-read it, and take another breath and let it sink in again.

If you think about it, in the midst and aftermath of what we experience as horrible events, doesn't great love and compassion, and spiritual inquiry arise at the same time? Doesn't it even seem to expand?

So, those are several possible perspectives that can maybe, partially explain the pain and suffering in the world, even though there is only a Source of well-being. The rest is a mystery from the limits of our human minds, and the messiness of life and change, and the need for contrast.

Now, holding these spiritual perspectives does not mean you won't feel compassion for people having their human experience, or that you won't take steps towards helping others and supporting change. When I coach people in pain, I do so from my greater spiritual knowing and powers. I know that their pain is their path to something better, and I *know* what they desire is possible. From that space, wonderful, positive changes happen for people so much more quickly and easily.

Perhaps as we learn as a species to live more from our Spirit-Selves, we will learn how to change and grow and allow our desires to manifest with less suffering. That's been my personal experience. I think this is a time of Awakening precisely for us to learn this. To awaken to who we truly are, and to live more from that perspective and those loving, creative powers. And the three doorways to the Soul are a wonderful means for doing so.

So, if you can more easily presuppose now that Source is only pure positive energy, and is always available for you to allow in, or not, or to use effectively, or not, how does that feel? For myself, I feel soothed by it, and safer. I can focus on my competency at being a master at allowing this good in, rather than fearing bad things that might happen from some external source.

In contrast, when you are perceiving life as only your smaller self, you might think something like, "The Universe is punishing me or teaching me a lesson." Or, "Evil spirits or bad energies are causing bad things to happen to me." Or, "I can be a victim in life, at the effect of circumstances."

How does this feel? Really feel this before continuing

Recall a time when you felt anxious in this way. Remember how that emotional guidance from Spirit felt, reminding you that you were not perceiving the situation from your Spirit-Self perspective.

The next time you feel that kind of fear or worry or anxiety, let those feelings be your reminder from Spirit to take a big, relaxing, centering breath, and to return to, "There is only a Source of well-being, and I either allow it in, or not."

Spirit is love-based. Everyone is perfect, worthy, and lovable as they are, *including me*. It is my birthright and it is a given.

You know how we feel about babies and young children? It's a given that they are perfect and lovable. Some of their *behaviors* may not be so likable, but we separate that from who they are. From Spirit's perspective, as "children of God", per se, it is the same for all of us *regardless of age*.

When we separate our behaviors from our being, we're less likely to characterize ourselves in negative ways that feel fixed. Instead, from a place of knowing that *who we are* is always lovable and worthy, we can focus on *how we behave,* which can change.

Think about it, if you *are* Spirit, how can you not be worthy of love? Is Spirit ever not worthy of love? Spirit IS love! What happens, however, is that we often forget this is who we are. We forget to see life through the perspective of Spirit; and the perspectives we slip into instead create problematic thoughts, feelings and behaviors.

Remember the indigenous tribe I mentioned earlier, that showers rule-breakers with love to heal them? They get this distinction. Their ritual is a way of trying to help that person return to love and wholeness; and *from that place, their behaviors will change, too.*

I can't even tell you how many people I've worked with who somehow learned as a child that they needed to be perfect or somehow earn the right to be loved. We just didn't know how to interpret the behaviors of the adults in our lives. We were scolded or punished for "bad" behaviors, or bad grades, and rewarded for the opposite. We were pressured to behave in certain ways for approval. Well, I bet you can come up with plenty of your own examples. What's a small kid to think?

From that limited level of development, of course we collapsed the two, thinking that how we behaved determined how we were loved. Of course, that wasn't really the case. Perhaps your *behaviors* weren't loved, but *you* most likely were loved unconditionally. And, regardless, from Spirit's perspective, you most definitely were perfect, worthy, and lovable.

Once my clients were able to accept this Spirit presupposition, along with some of the others coming up, they were able to love themselves and feel worthy of love again, which opened up a whole new world of possibilities for them, as you can imagine.

How does it feel when you hold this perspective? What does it open up for you?

In contrast, when you are perceiving life as only your smaller self, you might think something like, "I need to meet certain standards to be perfect and prove myself worthy of love and what I want."

Recall a time when you felt less than, or unworthy, or unlovable. Remember how that emotional guidance from Spirit felt, reminding you that you were not perceiving yourself from your Spirit-Self perspective.

The next time you experience something like this, let those feelings be your reminder from Spirit to take a big, relaxing, centering breath, and to return to, "Spirit is love-based. Everyone is perfect, worthy, and lovable as they are, including me. It is my birthright and it is a given."

Behind *every* behavior is a positive intention, no matter how evil, wrong, crazy, hurtful, or self-sabotaging it seems.

We've just talked about how it's useful to separate behavior from the person. This presupposition helps you understand behaviors even more deeply.

The motivation, or the concern behind all of your behaviors, including things you say, is to accomplish something positive for you. There's some part of you, usually subconscious, that believes that chosen behavior will take care of something it believes is important and needed for you. *That part is trying to take care of you.*

No matter how evil, crazy, hurtful, or self-sabotaging a behavior seems, that behavior is the best choice *perceived* as available to you at that point in time to take care of the positive intention it has for you.

I once had a client who drank wine every evening. It was becoming a problem for him in a number of ways, and he wanted to stop, but couldn't. We explored the underlying positive intention, and it was so he could relax. Once we became aware of this, we explored other ways to help him relax. He discovered that part of the relaxation came from the ritual itself and the permission he was giving himself to relax. It wasn't just the alcohol. He then began using a wine glass with something other than alcohol, and that, together with the same ritual and inner permission and awareness of it being his time to relax, worked!

When I was doing my Inner Way Weight Loss group, a lot of the women in it were moms – very tired moms. A lot of them struggled with unhealthy snacking, especially at night, and couldn't stop themselves. It seemed like self-sabotage. We explored the positive intentions, and for most of them, the intention was to relax and to treat themselves. All of the day, they were doing for others and working hard, and they wanted a treat to do something for themselves.

Unfortunately, that behavioral choice had negative consequences, just like wine drinking did for my other client. But, once they focused on the underlying positive intention, they were all able to come up with better, healthier, and even more satisfying ways to take care of the intention.

Some other examples of possible positive intentions are: yelling to be acknowledged/heard, smoking to relax, bullying to feel powerful, and procrastinating to relax or do something more appealing.

Keep in mind, that the positive intentions behind behaviors can be very individual. There are some pretty common ones, but it's not necessarily always the same for everyone. Even for you, it can vary at different times and contexts. For example, why you want to put something off one day can be different than on another day. You need to check within each time.

To uncover a positive intention for yourself or someone else, ask any of these questions:

- "What could doing this behavior be doing positively for me/you?"
- "What do I/you want by doing this behavior?"
- "What am I/you trying to take care of, that feels even more important, by doing this behavior?"
- "If I/you weren't doing this, what would I/you be missing out on?"

It's really important to use language that articulates what that part *does* want, versus what it doesn't want. For example, the positive intention of yelling might be t*o be heard, rather than* not to be ignored. Or, the positive intention of smoking or snacking or drinking might be *to relax*, rather than not to feel stressed any longer. The positive intention of procrastinating might be *to relax or to have some fun*, rather than to not work. Keep it in positive language. We'll be discussing this more later.

Remember, from the previous presupposition of Spirit, the positive worth of an individual is held constant. The value and appropriateness of the behavior are what's *questioned, but not judged or condemned;* because rather than just condoning or condemning one's actions, we can now also explore the positive intent behind the behavioral choice, and presuppose that there always is one.

When parents push their children to behave a certain way, it's because they love them and believe those behaviors will ensure their safety, or success, or well-being in some way- something they consider important. And, those behavioral choices they use are the only ones they know or perceive as possible for taking care of those underlying concerns.

Understanding the positive intention allows you to come up with more choices for taking care of that intention, or concern. It also allows you to have more understanding, compassion, and patience for yourself, and others.

Can you also see now that there really is no such thing as "self-sabotage", as if there's a part of you trying to make you fail, or as if you have an inner enemy? *Instead, know now that every part of you is always looking out for you.* Even choices that seem like they are intended to make you fail, have a positive intention behind them. For example, maybe there's a part of you that believes your success in something would have other negative consequences, like losing friends. So, the positive intention of having you fail would be to make sure you have friends.

If you recognize that there's a positive intention behind *every* behavior you and others choose, how does that feel? What changes for you?

One thing it does for me is it makes me feel like every person is inherently good inside; and I like how that feels.

In contrast, when you are perceiving life as only your smaller self, you might think something like, "Sometimes people have negative intentions."

How does that feel in comparison to presupposing there's a positive intention?

Recall a time when you judged yourself or someone else based on a behavior. Remember how that emotional guidance from Spirit felt, reminding you that you were not perceiving the situation from your Spirit-Self perspective.

The next time you experience something like this, let those feelings be your reminder from Spirit to take a big, relaxing, centering breath, and to return to, "Behind every behavior is a positive intention, no matter how evil, crazy, hurtful, or self-sabotaging it seems."

Even with awareness of the underlying positive intention, why would anyone choose a behavior that has negative consequences or is even ineffective? Read on to the next presupposition.

People always make the best choice available to them. Including me!

The keyword here is "available". People always make the best choices *available* to them at the time, given their competencies, their unique mental programs, and their automatic interpretations of the situation (even tho' there are often lots of better ones they're not aware of).

Similar to how computers have programming, so do we. Our thoughts, behaviors, and choices are primarily driven by our past conditioning, what we learned in our past. What we learned, however, was based on the level of understanding and interpretations we were able to make at the time.

Most of our beliefs were formed before we were six years old; and how is a young child able to interpret everything it sees and hears from that level of development!? Many of us interpreted how we were spoken to, or the school grades we received, or things like not being picked for a team, as not being good enough or needing to be perfect, or something similarly feeling unworthy and unlovable. And, that belief will continue to drive many choices and behaviors, and reactions throughout your life, if the belief is never addressed. We'll address beliefs later in the book. For now, just be aware that we are essentially bio-computers operating from the programs we each uniquely have. The programs can be changed and updated and added to; but, whatever it is at any moment in time is what you have to work with. Just like with a computer.

So, if you can't expect a computer to operate outside of its programming, perhaps it's not reasonable to expect people to operate outside of their current programs, either. It's the same phenomenon, after all.

Based on their understanding and perception of something, their belief in what they are capable of and what choices are possible for them, and their current capabilities, Spirit lovingly presupposes that people are always making the best choice *they perceive* they have or are capable of. Spirit accepts where you're at, and loves you unconditionally.

As Oprah Winfrey always says, "When you know better (or differently), you do better (or differently)."

For example, remember the women I mentioned earlier who wanted to lose weight but couldn't control their snacking and eating habits? They consciously knew they needed to make better choices, yet still didn't. Why? Because the underlying positive intention was operating more powerfully out of their awareness. It was a program running that limited their choices.

I also had a client who was struggling with her relationship with her brother, and she was really suffering about it. He kept making choices that she thought were bad ones, and they would argue about them to the point of him no longer wanting to even talk to her. She also tried to offer suggestions and support lovingly, but behind that, she was still feeling like he should know and do better. She held those judgments; and, he felt them. He might have even been judging himself, and been feeling bad about himself, too; but he wasn't able to change.

Once she understood this presupposition, that he was always making the best choices available to him according to his programming, she shifted to sincere compassion and understanding. Their relationship was mended. From there, there was a better chance of her being able to help him, or of him being open to getting help from a professional.

Usually, people are unaware of why they are making certain choices that don't serve them, and they are often unhappy and frustrated with themselves for making them. Have you felt this way before? Understanding the dynamic in this presupposition, however, will open you up to being more compassionate with yourself, and to getting support for changing beliefs and programs that get in the way of your desires. After you've completed this book, you'll also have strategies for doing this yourself.

This is an opportunity to see how making others and yourself wrong is unproductive, because if they, or you, could do differently, they, and you, would! This includes your parents, by the way! When you make someone wrong, you often get a protective or defensive reaction. Instead, open a conversation to explore the positive intention or beliefs or running perceptions behind the behavior. Bringing an inner narrative about the situation into awareness can be a great step. More on this later, too!

If you hold the perspective of Spirit, and presuppose that everyone is making the best choice available to them, including you, how does that feel? What changes for you?

In contrast, when you are perceiving life as only your smaller physical self, you might think something like, "Even though people might know better, they might still intentionally not do better. Self-sabotage is possible." Or, "People should know better, and if they don't, they should at least listen to me."

What does it typically mean about someone if they intentionally make a choice that's not the best choice for them? The common tendency is that it makes them wrong and stupid. However, this is NOT Spirit's perspective.

Recall a time when you judged yourself or someone else based on a behavior or choice that was made. Remember how that emotional guidance from Spirit felt, reminding you that you were not perceiving the situation from your unconditionally loving, Spirit-Self perspective.

The next time you experience something like this, let those feelings be your reminder from Spirit to take a big, relaxing, centering breath, and to return to, "People always make the best choice available to them. Including me!"

There is no failure. An unwanted experience is only feedback for more learning and growth, and to create newly.

Imagine you had a real Genie in a bottle, and you could always make another wish, or change your wish, or make adjustments to the wish that was "granted". Wouldn't that be nice? Would you be afraid of making the "wrong" wish, or of making mistakes? No, because you could always create newly!

Well, I have good news for you. YOU are the genie. YOU are the creator. And, it isn't rubbing the bottle that makes the wish come true. It's the asking, and fully expecting.

The thought of getting something right or wrong typically feels very permanent, doesn't it? However, if you truly hold yourself as being all-creative Spirit, would you feel this way? Try it on and see.

Spirit came into our diverse human experiences planning on having unwanted experiences; because from those, new desires and growth would be born. And, from those new desires, there would be new creations and, thus, expansion. If we never felt the temporary discomfort of something unwanted, we might not want something new.

Let's use children as an example. When they're learning, they make plenty of mistakes. They make their attempts pretty much fearlessly; and when they fall or don't get what they want, they merely try and try and try again. And, they usually do so with delight! They hold that state of wonder and joy in the process. They're still living very much as their Spirit-Selves. You can see it, and feel it. I'm inviting you to return to this state, and to return to this perspective of life being a series of learning adventures and desires fulfilled, knowing your creative powers and who you really are.

Every so-called "failure", including your desires not being fulfilled, is an opportunity to reveal how you're not allowing in what you desire, how you need to adjust your "tuning in" to "the station you want to listen", and to achieve more clarity, so your life can get better and better!

Each "failure" and unfulfilled desire is a GIFT, with a hidden limiting belief inside for you to breakthrough, and the opportunity to expand more into your Spirit-Self perspective!

With each so-called "failure", you can say to yourself, "I'm getting closer and closer!", and shift into a state of wonder, "I wonder how I can adjust my thinking and/or my behavior to manifest what I want?"

Does that feel better than, "Damn! I failed again! Where did I go wrong? I don't know what else to do!"

You have an opportunity to expand through *everything* you go through; and, like an artist who loves to create, Spirit revels in it all.

If you hold this perspective of Spirit, and presuppose that every unwanted experience is merely feedback, and that you always get to create newly and get better and better, how does that feel? What changes for you?

In contrast, when you're perceiving life as only your smaller physical self, you might think something like, "I need to get this right, or else (something bad) might happen.", or "If I get this wrong, it could be final, or irreparable.", or "I'm so mad at myself for doing that!"

Recall a time when you've experienced a similar fear or regret. Remember how that emotional guidance from Spirit felt, reminding you that you were not perceiving the situation from your Spirit-Self perspective.

The next time you experience something like this, let those feelings be your reminder from Spirit to take a big, relaxing, centering breath, and to return to, "There is no failure, only feedback. I am a creator, and I can always create newly! Every experience is an opportunity for learning and growth and my life getting better and better!"

Learning and life is an ongoing creative process; therefore, I will never be "done".

As I've mentioned, we are here in human form for Spirit to create through us, more and more and more and more and more! "Abraham" has said, "More is the mantra of the Universe. More please! I'll have some of that please!"

The grand design, so to speak, is for continual, never-ending expansion. To have never-ending desires and to have those desires fulfilled, and for life to get better and better. Well, how fun-sounding is all of that! Why would you want to be "done" with that?

We small-minded humans really like the idea of finally "getting it", or finally being complete in some way. We want to become enlightened and then we're good! And, because we have this striving, we work hard for it and sometimes even stress over the process or over taking too long or never getting there. You know that feeling?

But, that's not the design. So, you'll get that feeling sometimes of finally achieving what you want; and then, you won't. You'll think you're regressing or failing somehow, forgetting that everything is just feedback for more learning and growth and the next level of better. Nothing in life is static, even if it appears that way to our limited senses. In actuality, everything is always changing and in a cycle of change, as I discussed earlier in the book.

So, you can stop trying to be done, or complete, or perfect. That's not why you're here. Instead, embrace the ongoing adventure towards better and better and better! Whoopee!

If you hold this perspective of Spirit, and presuppose that you're not supposed to reach some end goal; and instead your life is an ongoing process towards better and better, how does that feel? What changes for you?

In contrast, when you're perceiving life as only your smaller physical self, you might think something like, "I need to get this already! What's taking me so long?" or, "I think I've finally got it! I've mastered this."

Recall a time when you've experienced a similar impatient or frustrated feeling. Remember how that emotional guidance from Spirit felt, reminding you that you were not perceiving the situation from your Spirit-Self perspective.

The next time you experience something like this, let those feelings be your reminder from Spirit to take a big, relaxing, centering breath, and to return to, "Life is an on-going, creative process; and I will never be done. It's a never-ending adventure of better and better and better!"

The Universe operates through dynamic exchange. As I give, I receive.

Have you noticed that what goes up, must come down? And have you noticed the natural flow of waves and tides coming in and going out?

How about all the examples of flow in your body: your circulatory system, your digestive system, and so on? There will always be an ebb and flow. A coming in, a going out, and a coming back in.

Energy needs to flow. When we stop the flow, problems arise, like stagnation, even constipation!

I find it really interesting that the Latin root of the word currency, is "currere", which means to run or to flow. And, that another word for money is currency!

Think about this, too. In this paradigm we're working with, *everything*, including human beings, is energy, We are electric! And, another word we use for electricity is currency!

Where am I going with this? This dynamic of flow and exchange applies to everything! It applies to all forms of giving and receiving. As you freely give joy, you'll receive joy. As you freely give love, you'll receive love. And, as you spend money believing in the flow of abundance, you can trust it will flow back to you.

I remember a time in our life when each month, according to math, our bills often totaled more than the income we knew for certain would be coming in. I kept a blank bank check over that list of bills with "paid in full" written on it, and always held the thought, "One way or another, what we need will be taken care of." And, it always was, and always has been! Just *know, from the knowing in your Soul,* that this is how the Universe works, *when you trust in and believe it.*

I'm not suggesting that if you barely have enough money in your account to pay your bills, that you go out and run up your credit card, or go spend it all on unnecessary things. The difference is in the mindset from which you make your choices. From a scarcity mindset, you might "withhold" your money because you "don't have enough" or because you feel poor. From the perspective of your Spirit-Self, you might choose to spend your money on your bills and not other things, while feeling abundant in doing so, feeling grateful to be able to do so, feeling happy to pay for what you have received and to give to those who provided it all, and know that more abundance will flow to you. As you do that, it will improve more and more, in delightful, even surprising ways.

The author and spiritual "guru" of Japan, Ken Honda, created a mantra for welcoming money into your life when you spend money with an open heart. Arigato is Japanese for thank you. He suggests that when you spend money, you say "Arigato in, arigato out", reminding yourself of the flow of abundance in life. I actually say it the other way around when I spend money or pay bills. "Arigato out, arigato in!"

From Spirit's perspective, abundance and flow are a given. Our true nature is one of affluence and abundance, because Nature/Source supports every need and desire. We are creators, and our essential nature is one of pure potentiality and infinite possibilities!

Doesn't that feel good? Try it on.

In contrast, when you're perceiving life as only your smaller self, you might think something like, "If I give or spend, I'll have less. I need to keep what I get. I may not have enough. I might run out." With regard to giving something of yourself, you might think something like, "I give, give, give, and I get nothing/so little in return!" This is all scarcity thinking and is not the perspective of Spirit. When you trust in the true nature of flow and dynamic exchange, you will create and attract it. When you have scarcity-based thoughts, you create and attract that.

Recall a time when you felt fearful about not having enough or not having the abundance or love, or joy, or whatever you desire. Remember how that emotional guidance from Spirit felt, reminding you that you were not perceiving the situation from your Spirit-Self perspective.

The next time you experience something like this, let those feelings be your reminder from Spirit to take a big, relaxing, centering breath, and to return to, "My true nature is one of affluence and abundance, because Nature/Source supports every need and desire. I am a creator, and my essential nature is one of pure potentiality and infinite possibilities! The Universe also operates through dynamic exchange. As I give, I receive! Thank you, thank you!"

Source/Nature's intelligence functions with effortless ease. Therefore, when I am aligned with Source, in states of harmony, love, and joy, I can accomplish what I want with ease.

Spirit is the creator of *all that is.* All that is! Do you think this powerful consciousness works hard to do so? Is it using effort? It's almost laughable to think of such a thing. The only reason we think creating what we want is going to be hard and that we have to put a lot of effort into it is because we forget that we are Spirit, and don't act from that way of being.

"No pain, no gain" or, *"Just do it!" are sayings that have* been heavily conditioned into us. Working hard, long hours is often considered to represent your success and value. No one ever rewards you for doing your job easily!

When you're living your life, or responding to a situation, from your Spirit perspective, in states of harmony, love, and joy, everything happens more harmoniously and easily. When you think as Spirit, you create as easily and powerfully as Spirit.

Here's a testimonial that relates to this, from a business owner who was one of our group program participants:

"I had been using Law of Attraction, but I was only getting "okay" results. I still had the belief that I had to work hard to get money. I was successful, but I worked hard for it. Then, for various reasons, work started cutting back; and I

realized I had to do something different or work harder. Since I shifted my belief about needing to work hard and learned how to get in "the zone" easier and easier, business picked up again. I even had my best day ever today.

I'm much more aware of my feelings and am easily able to shift them when I need to. Whereas before I might have been pissed about something all day; now I can shift within minutes. And from there the day just seems to get easier and easier. My mood is different, people in my life seem to be different, my employees seem to be more positive, and more business is coming my way. And the only thing I changed is how I look at things and what story I'm telling."

When I feel myself struggling or working hard, or thinking that I'll have to work hard, I now notice those unpleasant feelings that show up from those thoughts, and let them remind me to openly ask, *"How can this be easy?"* The magic that happens thereafter is so much fun! I get how this is all a fun game for Spirit! When we needed a new car (or whatever), it showed up and processed with ease. When I needed a new caretaker for my elderly parents, each step that was needed seemed to happen totally by surprise, and with almost effortless ease! I could go on and on. This is really worth playing with!

I'm not saying that you'll never have to put any work into anything. I put some work time into writing this book, as an example. However, when you hold the space of Spirit, it won't feel like work and it will go more easily than when you don't. When I had writing sessions in which I wasn't connected, and tried to force the writing from my head alone, it was never as easy, or as good, as when I took the time to connect to my whole self, and just let the book be written through me. How you think about what you do or need to do, will have a great impact on how it feels for you and how easily it will unfold. Even housework. Even medical procedures. Everything.

If you hold this perspective of Spirit and presuppose that you can accomplish or receive what you want with ease, how does that feel? What changes for you?

In contrast, when you're perceiving life as only your smaller physical self, you might think something like, "Ugh. This is going to be hard. It's going to take work and be unpleasant, and I don't want to do it!" "Guess I just have to dig my heels in and do it!"

Recall a time when you've experienced a similar feeling of dread or negative anticipation. Or recall a time when you became aware of how you were efforting your way through something. Remember how that emotional guidance from Spirit felt, reminding you that you were not perceiving the situation from your Spirit-Self perspective.

The next time you experience something like this, let those feelings be your reminder from Spirit to take a big, relaxing, centering breath, and to return to, "I am Source Energy, and I can accomplish what I want with ease!"

There is no death. I am an eternal being. My body will die, but the energy and Soul aspect of who I am will not. I will become just pure, positive Spirit consciousness again.

Do you remember the three levels of consciousness discussed in chapter one?

- Level one: "I am human. I *am* my body."
- Level two: "I am human, and I *have* a spirit, or Spirit/the Universe exists."
- Level three: "I am Spirit, and I have a human body."

If you indeed believe that you are Spirit having your physical, human experience, does it seem possible that the greater Spirit aspect of who you are would die when your body dies? Of course not. Spirit is eternal! If Spirit, the Source of all that is, ceased to exist, then life would cease to exist!

Even science has shown that energy cannot be destroyed, only transformed. And, even though we *perceive* ourselves as physical rather than energy, in actuality, what we're perceiving is really just energy.

When the form of your body "dies", you will then just be the pure Spirit consciousness that has always been the greater part of who you are. And, without your human mind thinking and creating from its automatic, conditioned programs, you will only experience the pure love, ultimate joy, and inner peace, and all the perspectives experienced as Spirit. From reports of people who have had near-death experiences (technically dead for a short time, and then came back to life), it is an experience beyond what our language can express. Perhaps this is what religions have attempted to express with the concept of heaven.

Additionally, when a person transitions back into pure Spirit, they are still available to you in that form. Many people have experienced this new form of connection. When Jerry Hicks died, after some time of adjusting, Esther, his wife, learned to focus on where he now *was*, rather than where he *wasn't*; and since then she has had a regular, easy connection and communication with him.

When we think of ourselves at only the first level of consciousness, as only bodies, it's easy to fear death and to be sad about it for ourselves and others. From that perspective, death is an ending. There's nothing. However, from this new perspective, death is a return to an even better experience. For now, we can only imagine it, and have faith in it; but it's a belief I find useful and therefore choose.

If you hold this perspective of Spirit and presuppose that when someone's body dies, the person returns to the blissfulness of pure love, ultimate joy, and infinite peace beyond what words can express, how does that feel? What changes for you?

In contrast, when you're perceiving life as only your smaller physical self, you might think something like, "When we die, it's over. There's just nothing." "When my loved one dies, they're gone."

Recall a time when you've experienced a similar thought. Remember how it felt, and how that emotional guidance from Spirit felt, reminding you that you were not perceiving the situation from your Spirit-Self perspective.

The next time you experience something like this, let those feelings be your reminder from Spirit to take a big, relaxing, centering breath, and to return to, "We are all eternal Source Energy; and when our bodies cease to exist, we return to pure love, joy, and peace beyond what words can express. And, when someone no longer physically exists in my reality, they are still available to me in their non-physical form, if I allow it."

The purpose of life is JOY, and life is supposed to be FUN! That is why I am here.

This might be challenging for some to accept because there are so many teachings that say we each have a more specific purpose to fulfill, and that we're here to serve others.

But consider this, when you're *not* experiencing joy in what you're doing, and you feel some other undesirable emotion instead of joy, what is that emotional guidance telling you? It's your reminder that you're not holding your greater Spirit-Self's perspective! *And, Spirit's perspective always feels good.*

From Spirit's perspective, human life is all just a big playground and adventure. Like when we go to the movies, or an amusement park, or play your favorite sport or game, or do your favorite hobby, or listen to your favorite music, and so on. You just step in and out of various, temporary experiences for the fun of the experience. Even when it's a scary or sad movie, you enjoy the experience, knowing it's not real and not permanent; and you leave saying, "That was good!". Have you had an experience like that?

For me, when I focus on what feels good for me, or find a way to feel good about something that doesn't automatically have appeal to it, what feels "right" for me shows up. I sense what I'm "meant" to do and feel drawn to it, and it often involves helping others. But there's no rule about it, and no "shoulds" about it. It's all driven by my connection to my Spirit-Self, which then directs me to joy.

Yes, there are things we just "have" to do. For example, to be honest with you, the process of sitting at my computer writing this book was not always "fun". My bum got tired and it took more patience than I was often feeling. However, I focused on *why* I was writing the book, and the value it would be creating for each person who read it. That always felt exciting! I continuously felt my inner tug to complete it. And each time I finished writing a segment, I felt great joy!

What if you could find a way to feel good even about the things you "have" to do? As we continue in the book, we'll be discussing how to tell better-feeling stories. For now, just experiment with the various Spirit perspectives, and see how that helps.

If you hold the perspective of Spirit that the purpose of your life is joy, and you're here to have fun, how does that feel? What changes for you?

In contrast, when you're perceiving life as only your smaller physical self, you might think something like, "I don't know why I'm here. What's it all about beyond surviving? It's not supposed to be fun. There's no virtue in that.", "Sometimes you just have to suffer through it."

Recall a time when you've experienced a similar thought. Remember how it felt, and how that emotional guidance from Spirit felt, reminding you that you were not perceiving the situation from your Spirit-Self perspective.

The next time you experience something like this, let those feelings be your reminder from Spirit to take a big, relaxing, centering breath, and to return to, "The purpose of life is JOY, and life is supposed to be FUN! That is why I am here."

Summary list of the presuppositions of Spirit

Feel free to re-word these in your own way that is easy for you to remember and use. And, if you forgot what one means as you read it, go back and re-read about it again.

1. "I am Spirit, and I have a body."
2. I am a creator!
3. Unlimited abundance and possibilities for accomplishing my desired outcomes are available to me.
4. Uncertainty means unlimited possibilities are still available.
5. I can be, do, or have anything I desire. And, I have all I need within me to be the creator of and have the solutions for all I desire.
6. I am responsible for my experience. Everything I experience is a reflection of my vibration, thoughts, and focus.
7. "Ask and you shall receive." Inherent within every intention and desire are the mechanics for their fulfillment.
8. I allow others their experience because as Source/Spirit, there is no right or wrong; and it's an all-inclusive Universe.
9. There is only a Source of well-being, and I either allow it or not.
10. Contrast, diversity, and polarities are all part of the process of creation and growth, and evolution, personally and collectively. Therefore, I can accept and even appreciate all of it. All is well from this perspective.
11. Spirit is love-based. Everyone is perfect, worthy, and lovable as they are, *including me*. It is my birthright and it is a given.
12. Behind *every* behavior is a positive intention, no matter how evil, crazy, hurtful, or self-sabotaging it seems.
13. People always make the best choice available to them. Including me!
14. There is no failure. An unwanted experience is only feedback for more learning and growth, and to create newly moving forward.
15. Learning and life is an ongoing creative process; therefore, I will never be "done".

16. The Universe operates through dynamic exchange. As I give, I receive.
17. Source/Nature's intelligence functions with effortless ease. Therefore, when I am aligned with Source, in states of harmony, love, and joy, I can accomplish what I want with ease.
18. There is no death. I am an eternal being. My body will die, but the energy and Soul aspect of who I am will not. I will become just pure, positive Spirit consciousness again.
19. The purpose of life is JOY, and life is supposed to be FUN! That is why I am here.

Exercise for practicing the perspectives of Spirit

So far, you've been reading about and imagining how holding the perspectives of Spirit makes a difference in how you feel and what you thus experience. Now it's time to start practicing, so you can increase your level of awareness of who you're being in the moment, and begin to develop new ways of thinking that will support you in living the life of increasing inner peace, love, ease, and joy that you came here for.

Without practice, this is all potentially just information that won't get embodied and used. The few minutes it takes to practice and to learn is no big deal, unless you make it so. I'm sure, like me, you do many other things that have less return on your few minutes of time investment. Based on the experiences of the many people I've guided through this, I think you'll find it easy, and interesting, and very worthwhile!

You can do this process by just sitting and using your imagination. However, if you want it to have an even greater impact, I suggest you do the standing and moving version as I describe it. Doing this uses more of your neurology, and builds new neural networks more quickly. Up to you.

The steps are written out for you here. I've also provided a recording of me guiding you through it. With just a little practice, you'll easily be able to use this process on your own. It's essentially the same as the "Re-Sourcing" process we did in the previous chapter, now adding the Spirit perspectives, or presuppositions, that you just learned in this chapter.

Before you begin, I recommend having your recap list of the Spirit perspectives available to look at, as you'll be using it in this exercise. You might want to take a little time someday to type and print them up for easy access and visibility. Doing this will also help you remember them.

Begin by standing, leaving enough room behind you to take a few steps back.

1. Think of a situation or context in which you act more as only your smaller, human self, and you're not as resourceful, or behaving or responding you'd like. Examples: wanting to behave differently, or dealing with or responding to others in a way you're not pleased with, or wanting to feel differently about a particular concern. Be sure to actually come up with something before continuing.

2. Recall the who, what, where, and when that this happens, so you can re-create it and associate into it, which means to *fully experience and feel it in your body as if it's happening now.* You don't want to be seeing or observing yourself. You want to be re-experiencing it.
    - What emotions are coming up for you? How do you feel? Do you feel some version of confusion ("I don't know what's going on and I don't like it.")? What else?
    - How is your body feeling in response to those emotions? How is your breathing? Do you feel tension anywhere? What about your posture? What else are you noticing physically? The more you become aware of how you're feeling and the feedback you're being given, the more likely you'll also notice them in real life, or real time.

- What thoughts are you having that are creating these responses? Take your time to become aware of them. This is a critical step.

This is you being your "smaller self", thinking through that historically conditioned, limited perspective.

3. Leave the feelings you were having in that location, and take a few steps back from where you were standing. "Shake off" the feelings, literally shaking your arms and body about, and shift into perplexity, curiously asking, "Who am I being? What is my emotional guidance telling me?" (Remember, if you don't feel good, your guidance is reminding you that you're holding a different perspective than your greater Spirit-Self. You're feeling that inner conflict or incongruency.)

4. Take a few big, relaxing, centering breaths from your lower belly; *and expand into your whole Spirit-Self again, "Re-Sourcing"*, so you can feel calm, resourceful, and open to your greater Spirit perspective. To help you re-create this state, you might also want to use the "anchors" or associations you created earlier in the "Box into Spirit and Re-Sourcing" meditation.

5. From the list of presuppositions of Spirit, find one or more that would be a more helpful way to think about your problem situation. If you're not sure which ones, just try a few that you intuitively feel drawn to trying.

6. Fully take on each presupposition you've chosen, as if it were really true. Then look at yourself in the "small self" context in front of you through the filter of the presupposition of your Spirit-Self. See your smaller self through the eyes of your greater Spirit Self, holding this Spirit perspective. So, for example, if you chose the presupposition "Everyone is doing the best they're able to/making the best choice available to them in any moment in time.", you would hold this perspective

as you look at your smaller-self in front of you in the problem context.

7. Still holding the presupposition, step forward into the "small self" location again, *bringing this Spirit-Self way of thinking and the resources that come with it with you into that previously problematic situation.*
What happens?
   - What shifts in your thinking?
   - What shifts in your possibilities?
   - Do you feel differently emotionally or physically?
   - How do you want to respond in that situation now?

8. Imagine a time coming up in the future when this type of situation might present itself again, and mentally rehearse and imagine your new way of thinking and responding.

9. If you feel it might be helpful, repeat steps 4 - 7 with other relevant Spirit presuppositions, until you feel satisfied.

I encourage you to repeat this process with other "small self" situations you'd like to overcome and change.

Another way of doing this exercise is to write each presupposition on a piece of paper and place them in a large circle around you. You imagine your problematic, small-self with a specific issue while in the center; and then step into each presupposition to try them on and see if they make a difference.

Here's how you can use this shifting process in any moment during your day:

1. When you don't feel good either emotionally or in your body (shallow breathing, tension, etc.), these are your cues/emotional guidance that you're thinking from only your smaller human-self perspective and not your *much* greater Spirit-Self.

2. When you notice this, shift into perplexity or wonder, asking "Who am I being? What is my emotional guidance telling me?"

3. Take a big, relaxing, expanding centering breath; *and expand into your whole Spirit-Self again,* so you can feel calm, resourceful, and open to a different perspective again- your greater Spirit perspective.

4. Think of one or more Spirit perspectives that would be helpful. Sometimes, as soon as you center and expand, the appropriate perspectives will show up. The more often you practice feeling yourself as Spirit, through meditation and centered breathing, the more often this will happen.

5. Bring this Spirit-Self way of thinking and the resources that come with it with you into your situation.

Recap and practice

You've now learned and experienced that you don't have to be at the effect of your circumstances. The circumstances themselves aren't creating how you feel and respond. It's your thinking that is doing it. As you learn to center, relax and expand into your Whole Spirit-Self, and use your doorway of language to adjust your thinking to be more aligned with Spirit's perspectives, your experiences will change in positive ways, as well!

Commit to be mindful of the doorways of your emotions and body – how you feel physically and emotionally from moment to moment. And, if you don't feel good, take a few big, relaxing, centering breaths, and like in the Box into Spirit meditation, expand into your full Spirit-Self. Then you'll more easily be able to shift your thinking from your small-self perspective to that of your greater, whole, Spirit-Self.

As an extension of Spirit, you have the resources you need available within you, and you can bring them forth. It's just a matter of shifting your focus to the space of who you really are, and the resources and better-feeling thoughts will be there. As we continue, you'll learn even more strategies for easily doing this.

I suggest you review the Spirit presuppositions at least once a day by reviewing the summary list, and practice shifting to Spirit perspectives at least once a day, as well. You can do this either by recreating a situation, like in the exercise, or by doing it in the moment when a situation shows up and your body and emotions provide indicators (feedback and guidance) that you're not holding Spirit perspective.

The goal is to live with this kind of moment-to-moment mindfulness, and to easily shift to Spirit perspective in the moment when needed. And then, the more you do this, the more and more you will move through your day from your Spirit perspective in the first place, needing to shift less and less often, and living with more and more inner peace, love, ease, and joy.

Guided Meditations for continuing your practice of experiencing yourself as Spirit:

For a slideshow with images and summaries of all the Spirit perspectives, go to www.newpossibilitiescoaching.com/three -doorways-to-the-soul-book.html

For a guided recording of the exercise for practicing the perspectives of Spirit, go to www.newpossibilitiescoaching .com/three-doorways-to-the-soul-book.html.

"I am here": In this meditation, we practice feeling present, being "here"; and we also practice creating a sense of the presence of Spirit within and all around us.

To listen to this guided meditation, go to www.newpossibilities coaching.com/three-doorways-to-the-soul-book.html.

Meditation with one-word mantras, like peace, love, and thank you: This keeps meditation nice and simple; yet, through the power of language and your focus, you'll create and experience beautiful feelings of peace, love, and gratitude, which are all experiences of Spirit.

I didn't record this meditation, as it is so simple to do on your own; and I want to encourage you to do so. Simply put on some meditation music, or, if you prefer, sit in silence; and after some relaxing breathing, simply repeat and reflect on one-word mantras like "peace", "love", or "thank you". I like to focus on repeating just one of them for a while, before moving on to another. And, of course, you can choose other words that work for you, as well.

CHAPTER FIVE

"Abracadabra!" I create as I speak!

The Doorway of Language

More on the doorway of language:

- How you create as you speak
- The difference between the problem frame and the outcome frame
- Setting your inner GPS with your intentions, language, and attention/focus
- Is it true?
- How to tell a better-feeling story
- Practicing the power of intention with the, "I am the Space for…" guided meditation

If you've been practicing the meditations and processes I've offered so far, you've begun to *feel* Spirit more and to understand the perspectives of Spirit. We've also raised your awareness of how your body and your emotions let you know who you're being at any moment in time, and how to return to your whole Self with centering and "Re-Sourcing" when needed. Now we're going to talk more about the importance of how you use language. *Whether you're speaking and thinking as your small self or your greater Spirit-Self will affect the experience you're having, and how effectively you'll create what you DO want, rather than what you don't want.*

There's a theory that the ancient Aramaic term "Abracadabra!" means

"I will create as I speak." And, so it is! Like magic! Your mind is like an inner GPS. It will go where you set your intentions and attention; and your experience will match your inner narratives (your thoughts, beliefs, and what you're saying to yourself). The evidence of your thinking shows up. I'm sure you've had experiences like this. For example, do you recall thinking about buying or doing something, and then you started seeing it everywhere? Like a certain kind of car, or a new hairstyle. They were always there; but then you started noticing them.

Try this. Close your eyes, and think of a color. Any color. Now open them and softly gaze around.

Did the color seem to show up and stand out, whereas before you hadn't really noticed it? It usually does.

From a law of attraction perspective, how you think and speak is like a GPS in that you are creating within the field of infinite potential through your thoughts and language. This is the language doorway to the Soul.

I remember a fun story a client excitedly shared with me one day after we had just talked about this principle. She was home, hungry for lunch, with no food in the house; and she had left her wallet at her business. She thought, "Wouldn't it be nice if some money showed up somehow by surprise." Just a little bit later, she was taking her clothes out of the dryer, and she found money that had been left in one of the pockets! She was SO delighted because she was experimenting with the magic possible with her speaking, and she got to experience it! I've received similar excited texts and emails from clients many times.

The quality of your life will depend on the quality of the conversations you have with yourself and others.

Let's begin with a little experiment.

THREE DOORWAYS TO THE SOUL

Think of something that is a mild problem for you in your life right now, like someone who annoys you, or something you're unhappy with, and answer the following questions. To get the full benefit, please actually think of something and actually answer the questions.

What's wrong? (What's your problem?)

Why is it a problem?

How does it limit you?

What caused it?

Whose fault is it?

How do you feel about your problem after answering those questions?

Now answer these questions, with the same problem:

> What's the essence of what you want instead?
>
> When you get what you want, what will it be like? Tell me as much detail as you can!
>
> When it happens, what else in your life will improve?
>
> What resources are available that might help you accomplish what you want?
>
> What else comes to mind that might support you in achieving your desire?
>
> What could this problem/experience be an opportunity for? How might it be happening for me/us?

What else is possible? How can this be even better?

How do you feel about your problem after answering those questions?

What was the emotional difference for you between answering the two sets of questions? Answer this before continuing.

The problem frame versus the outcome frame

The first set, called a *"**problem frame**"*, leaves most people feeling the same as they did before asking the questions, *or even worse*, perhaps stuck, confused, resigned, dispirited, limited, or something similar. It keeps you focused on what's wrong/the *problem*, and it doesn't really get you anywhere useful. Did you experience something like that?

The second set, called the *"**outcome frame**"*, gives you some direction, and is more likely to create a more positive mood. The **focus is on what you want**, and the questions and thoughts are *"**generative**"*. That is, they generate ideas, energy, and movement towards achieving your goal. This concept of being generative is always useful to keep in mind. *You want your thoughts, and your conversations with others, to generate a positive effect, versus a limiting one, or worse, one that stops you or others.* Think of it as being an engine generating movement versus being the brakes.

When you ask outcome, or solution-oriented, generative questions, you might not even have answers in the moment. You can just surrender them to the Universe/Spirit, and be open to receiving the answers and solutions. Rather than asking in a mood of need, it's a mood of openness, faith, and an invitation to receive what you're asking for.

Just before I started writing this book, I went to visit my 95-year-old parents in Florida. I had been speaking to them regularly on the phone and could tell that my mother's mental and physical health was declining. However, they kept reassuring me that they were doing fine and handling it all well enough.

When I got there, what showed up was very different than they'd led me to believe. Without going into the details, it was not good at all. It was chaos in many ways.

I went into an automatic survival mode, trying to physically do as much as I could to return the house and my mother to healthier conditions and to get some support for them. This involved a lot more than I could handle and I soon felt the physical and emotional stress and overwhelm.

Luckily, I soon recognized how I was feeling as guidance to listen to, that I was approaching all of the problems from only my small, physical, human perspective. I calmed myself down with some meditation and tapping (later in the book), and simply and openly asked, "What else is possible? How can this be better? How can this be easier?", "I invite this in."; and I surrendered it to the Universe.

From there on, it was a magical sequence of perfect synchronicity, lining up everything we needed with much greater ease. Months later still, as I'm writing this, everything is going really smoothly; and my Mom is also doing much, much better.

The problem frame and outcome frame show up in questions, and also in the conversations you have with others and yourself (your thoughts). The key is, which frame is your focus on.

Just becoming even minimally competent at observing when you, or another, are in the problem frame, and then *gently transitioning* into the outcome frame, will get you well on your way to being more satisfied and effective at getting what you want and in supporting others, as well.

Here's an example:

You: "Hi Joe. How you doing today?"

Joe: "Okay, but I'm working too much." (problem)

You: "And? " (asking for more information)

Joe: "Well, you know, no time for myself, or family, and I'm tired all the time. You know how it is." (problems)

You: "Yea, it's pretty common. So, what do you want instead?" (leading into the outcome frame)

Joe: "I'd like to work fewer hours!" (outcome/goal)

You: "Sounds good. Like how many, specifically?"

Joe: "The basic 40 would be nice."

You: "If you could work only 40 hours/week, what would change for you?"

Joe: "I wouldn't feel so tired and overwhelmed." (slipped back into problem frame)

You: "How would you rather feel?" (shifting back into outcome frame)

Joe: "Healthy and balanced." (And the process continues, for example, "How might you achieve this?")

If we return to the radio station analogy, staying in a problem frame is like tuning your radio into one station, yet still expecting to be able to hear another station that you really want to listen to. Why would you do such a thing!

It is WAY more common for people to focus on and talk about a problem, rather than the desired outcome and possible solutions. It's also a very,

very common way of relating socially. Venting with someone can have some emotional value, but leaving it at only that is limiting. Additionally, according to the law of attraction, you attract and create what you focus on. So, if you predominantly think and talk about the problem, which is what you *don't* want, what will you be perpetuating and attracting more of? The problem! You're still tuned in to the wrong radio station, and telling the Grand GPS where you DON'T want to go!

This is such a simple principle. Yet, because we've developed such ingrained habits of being problem-oriented, you'll need to set your intention to learn this new way of thinking and speaking. Fortunately, your emotional guidance will alert you to when you're in the problem frame because it generally doesn't feel good. Spirit is always solution-oriented; already orchestrating what you have asked for through your experience of the problem, and always calling you towards it. Focusing on only the problem will not feel good, because that's not Spirit's perspective. Your beautiful emotional guidance system is Spirit guiding you towards what you want!

Now, this does not mean that we stick our heads in the sand and ignore problems. Not at all. As Louise Hay used to say, we can't clean the house if we don't see the dirt. The difference is that focusing on the problem is only step one. We don't want to stay there and just complain about the dirt and keep expanding on how dirty the house is. Once we have the clarity for what we want and need instead, then it's time to move on.

So, remember, instead of only thinking about and talking about what's wrong; keep your focus on and talk about *what you want instead*. This is the beginning of you succeeding at anything you desire. Through this focus and alignment with Spirit, the path towards what you want will show up far more easily than staying more problem-oriented.

One of the easiest tips for doing this is to stop using the words don't, not, and no. There's a reason for this. If I were to tell you, "Don't think of an orange." What do you think of?

The orange! Right? When you use a GPS, you don't put in where you don't want to go, like, "Don't take me to Boston." How ridiculous! You put in where you DO want to go.

Let's try this again. "I don't want to eat junk food." Where did your inner GPS take you? Did you see junk food? Is that where you really wanted to go? Our minds don't really process negatives. Can you imagine, or see "don't"? But you can easily imagine "eat junk food". Right? If you don't want to eat junk food, what you actually DO want is to eat healthy food. Saying, "I want to eat healthy food." is more likely to get you there.

Here are some other common examples:

- "Don't forget...!" rather than "Please remember."
- "I don't want to get anxious." rather than "I want to stay confident and calm."
- "Don't talk to me that way." rather than "Please speak to me kindly/respectfully/softly."
- "Don't run!" rather than "Please walk!"
- "Don't be so loud!" rather than "Please be quieter."
- "Let's not - x -" rather than "Let's do - y - ."
- "Let's not be late." rather than "Let's be on time."
- "There will be no talking during the movie." rather than "Please be quiet during the movie."

Getting the idea? Similarly, be mindful of what comes to mind as you think about how to express what you want. For example, "I want to stop smoking/overeating/staying up too late, etc." Did using the word "stop" really express and bring your mind to what you DO want? Not likely. Something like, "I want to make healthy choices." would be more effective.

Similarly, if you were to say "I want to be less stressed and tired.", what do you end up thinking about? "I want to be more relaxed and have more energy." would be more effective at directing you towards what you want.

It would also serve you to refrain from saying, "I can't." These are some of the most self-limiting words you can use. There's a great quote by Henry Ford that explains why:

"Whether you think you can or you think you can't, you're right."

Your words and thoughts will shape the reality around you; and what you say, you will experience. So when you use the words "I can't," guess what? Most likely, you won't.

Best-selling author Jack Canfield does an experiment at his live events that proves this. He gets volunteers from the audience to stand up and extend an arm to their side. Then, Jack tells the volunteers to think either "I can" or "I can't." He then proceeds to push down on their arms, asking them to resist the pushing.

When he tries to push down the arms of the people who think "I can," their arms don't budge. Almost like they were made of concrete!

But when he tries to push down the arms of the people who think "I can't", they become so weak that he's able to push their arms down like a knife through butter. Have someone try this with you. You'll see for yourself how powerful your words and thoughts are.

How you word your thoughts and speaking will also affect how you feel. As an example, notice how each of these feels for you: "I am depressed." as compared to "I'm feeling depressed".

It's a subtle difference, isn't it; but it's significant. For most people, saying "I *am* (fill in the blank)." feels more fixed. Whereas, saying "I *feel* (fill in the blank)." feels more temporary, and like it can change.

The language you use in your thinking and speaking is very powerful, and is like magic. So, be mindful of the effect your wording has on the focus they create for you, and on how they make you feel. Then, adjust accordingly!

Using the power of intention

Have you ever experienced a time when you randomly thought of someone that you hadn't thought about in a long time, then your phone rings or they text you, and it's them?

William Tiller is a current renowned scientist who is a strong advocate for meditation, non-physical science, and spirituality. He has published over two hundred and fifty conventional scientific papers, three books, and several patents; and coined the term *Psychoenergetic Science* to describe his work that combines consciousness and science. He is convinced, as are many other scientists now, that, through an observable phenomenon called entanglement, our intentions can and do influence physical reality.

"For the last four hundred years, an unstated assumption of science is that human intention cannot affect what we call 'physical reality.' Our experimental research of the past decade shows that, for today's world and under the right conditions, this assumption is no longer correct. We humans are much more than we think we are and Psychoenergetic Science continues to expand the proof of it."

– Dr. William Tiller

Setting your intentions for something you want can be a very powerful, easy, and effective means of placing a request with the Universe, and for setting your personal "GPS". Used correctly, it will also seem like magic. You can use them to start your day, to prepare for a meeting or presentation, to prepare for a family gathering, or anything social, just about anything. Really! It's intentional creating for moving through your day.

We're still using the doorway of language; so, again, it's useful to be aware of what words work best for you. Try on each of these statements one at a time, *filling in the blank with something real for you, and notice how they each feel.*

- "I intend to (fill in the blank)." For example, "I intend to stay relaxed and calm today." or "I intend to finish my project today."
- "I will (fill in the blank)."
- "I want (fill in the blank)."
- "It's my intention to (fill in the blank)."
- "I invite in…"

For most people, the first three come more from the small-self and a place of will, as in willpower, force, and making it happen. And, when you say "I will", if you don't do what you said, it's more of a set-up for feeling like you've failed.

"It's my intention to…", or "I invite in…" as opposed to "I intend to" are less willful, and *partner with the Universe from a place of ease and trust* vs. making it happen or needing it to happen. The latter are not allowing states.

It's also really important to fully believe that what you're intending and asking for is possible. Words alone don't put out the vibrational signal to the Universe. *It's how the language you use makes you feel that creates your vibration.* If you don't believe in what you're asking for, inside you'll be going something like, "Um, I don't think so!" or "I wish!". It will be a negative, doubtful, or fearful feeling that is essentially like putting the brakes on at the same time you're trying to accelerate. What you're feeling and imagining could be stronger than what you're saying, and thus what you feel will get created instead!

If you're feeling any kind of doubt, one way around this is to use "I'm open and willing" statements.

- I'm open and willing to see everyone through my Spirit-Self perspective."
- I'm open and willing to be kind to my co-worker." (Who you usually find annoying)
- "I'm open and willing to receive (fill in the blank with your desire)
- "I'm open and willing to experience abundance today, and I invite that in."

How does "I'm open and willing to" feel for you? It makes whatever you're saying easier to believe, doesn't it? You're focusing on the potential, rather than it really happening. In this way, your "GPS" is still set in a believable way. I like to also add, "and I invite that in".

Another variation is "I am the Space for...." ("I am the space for more love, laughter, and friends." is one of my favorite intentions!) I've included an "I am the space for" guided meditation for you to enjoy.

I thought I would share my personal daily morning intentions that I use upon wakening. It sets a vibrational momentum for the day by reminding me of who I am and who and how I want to be throughout my day, vs. just what I want to accomplish or happen. In the end, I often set my more specific intentions for what I also want to do and accomplish, and imagine how I will feel at the end of my day having done them. But this is secondary to the other intentions. My intentions are a bit lengthy. They kind of grew over time. Yours can be as short or as long as you like.

"Abraham" (Consciousness/Spirit as channeled thru Esther Hicks) talks a lot about setting your vibrational momentum at the start of your day with whatever works for you: yoga, meditating, imagining, setting intentions, journaling, exercising, etc. I highly encourage you to get up early enough to allow yourself time to do some combination of these, as it is SO, SO worth it! You'll soon begin to notice the difference on the days that you skip it. Just my suggestion. Try it and see for yourself!

My basic template for my daily morning intentions (personalize it for yourself, of course)

Good morning day! I'm so happy and grateful for the gift of this day, and I expect good things. Surprise me, Universe! (Here I usually expand on what I feel grateful for and *really feel* it. "I'm so thankful for..., and I love...")

Today, as with every day, it's my dominant intent, that no matter what the circumstances, I will focus on positive aspects, and I will BE positive, kind, loving, present, patient, and accepting; and I will look for reasons to feel good and thoroughly enjoy my day.

It's my intention to remember and be all that I am. I am Ann Ide, *and so much more*. I am a physical extension of the Spirit consciousness and Source Energy of all that is, all-knowing, all-loving, all joy and peace, and the creative power of all that is; therefore it is all available to me. I am here for that greater part of me to create, express, expand, experience, and manifest through me, uniquely as me. And I was created with my unique traits as gifts for fulfilling my purpose in my unique way, to help others experience more inner peace, love, ease, and joy; and I invite that in.

I came for the fun and joy of being able to be, do and have all that I desire with ease and joy. I am a creator. All I have to do is ask, expect, and allow. (Here, I might let myself *feel* the fun of that, and the feeling of "Yes!" Yes! Let's go there! Yes! Let's do that! Yes! We can do that! Let me treat you! It's the feeling of total freedom to be, do and have all that I need and desire that I'm imagining.)

It's my intention to fully allow myself to experience all that I am and all that I came here for by maintaining a matching positive vibration of my greater Spirit-Self, and to allow the greater part of who I am to easily and fully speak and flow through me. To see, hear, feel, sense, think, speak and act from my greater Source-Self perspective; and to stay keenly aware of its ongoing presence and guidance in all forms within and around me in ways I can be easily aware of and understand, for the easy and joyful physical manifestation of all that I need and desire, to thoroughly enjoy the process and delightful unfoldings along the way, and to enjoy each and every moment by moment by moment, all with the highest good, health and well-being for all concerned. And so it is. Thank you, thank you, thank you.

Here's another example of my intentions before coaching, teaching, or leading a group:

First, I connect to and feel the field of Spirit as I ask my self, "Who am I?"; then I mindfully say,

"I am Ann Ide, and SO much more (meaning Spirit). It's my intention for my time with (person/group) to have all my skills, knowledge, and resources available to me, and especially to be Source-full. To fully allow all that I am (meaning Spirit) to easily and fully speak and flow through me, with all the love, connection (meaning to the person/people, and to Spirit), wit, wisdom, full presence, patience, playfulness, and easy, easy flow of having all the right things to ask, say, and do; with the centered, composed, confidence, competence, and creativity of all the masters and my greater Spirit-Self. So that by the end of our time together, they will have received and experienced exactly what they need in a positive, lasting way, and will leave feeling uplifted, inspired, and really, really good; and we will feel satisfied, fulfilled, and appreciative of our time together.

Lastly, here's a helpful checklist for effective intentions:

- Explore what language works for you as partnering with Spirit, rather than using "I will".
  Examples: "It's my intention…" or "I invite in…" vs. "I intend.." or "I will…"; "It's my desire/request…", I choose…", "I declare…" "I'm open and willing…", "I am the Space for…"

- Use language that is outcome-oriented and that helps you to imagine the outcome you desire, stating only what you do want, rather than what you don't want.

- Be sure you fully believe what you're saying. You should have no inner conflict or doubt about any of it. (More on this in the next segment of the book on "Telling a better-feeling story".)

- Consider using it for how you want to BE, not just what you want to accomplish or have.

- Before you begin, connect in some way to the space of peace and Spirit, or your heart. State your intentions from that state, not from your head alone.

- Really feel what you're saying, and imagine it as being done.

- Feel free to incorporate gratitude to raise your vibration. Again, really feeling it as you say it.

The one question that will set you free

Years ago, we were going to a family wedding in NH, somewhere we hadn't been to before. It was the early days of the GPS for cars. They weren't integrated into cell phones, yet, but were separate devices you connected in your car; and the maps the system used were not as accurate as they are now.

We were driving along, trusting the directions we were given by the GPS, and it took us to a dirt road in the woods. "Well, maybe the wedding is down here in some kind of nature setting!", we thought. But then the road became a more narrow, overgrown path; and it definitely felt wrong. Eventually, we could barely drive on it, and somehow found a way to do a three-point turn and go back.

We later found out that it used to be the main route to where we were going before a new road was built. The GPS maps just hadn't been updated. That old map was all the GPS had to operate from, and we trusted it as accurate.

Even though it made us late, Mark and I thought it was so funny; because we know that people operate in the same way, and it was a perfect analogy. Each of us has our own history and experiences that create conditioned programming, or "mental maps" of our reality, that we trust as true.

Remember when I discussed the presupposition that "Everyone is making the best choice they perceive as available to them."? I suggested the analogy that we are each like bio-computers, each with our own programming that we operate from.

We all interpret what we see, hear, and feel in any moment, in our own unique ways through our own unique programs. This becomes our experience of "reality", our own "map" of reality.

Key points to remember about this:

- Your mental maps of the world are not *the* world/reality. They are just *your map* of it.

- Accepting that we each create our own unique maps of reality, we can accept that *there is no one truth or reality within any experience.*

- Everyone's map is valid and true *to them*, given how they came to form it from their life experiences; and it needs to be respected as much as you want your own experience to be respected.

- Like our trip to NH, if you have an old, incomplete, or inaccurate map, you might have limited choices and possibilities. It's wise to be open to new maps and other interpretations.

From the programs, or maps, we have available, we interpret what we see, feel and hear, and then act from those interpretations. What can cause problems, is when we presuppose, usually unconsciously, they are *the truth*.

The difference between fact and interpretations

Imagine you're watching a professional tennis match with a friend. You love player A, and your friend loves player B. Player A hits the ball back to the other player. The ball hits the net and falls into player B's court, and player A wins the point. You exclaim, "Wow, that's skill!" Your friend disagrees, and says, "No way! That was just luck." What ensues is an argument over who is right, you or your friend.

So, who's right? What's true here?

What was true is that the ball hit the top of the net and it fell into player B's court, and player B lost the point. All the rest was each person's interpretation based on their mental maps and the standards they each held.

The important point here is that people are always collapsing facts with interpretations, and acting as if their interpretations are the truth.

Things, people, events, circumstances, etc. are not good or bad, nor do they have any meaning in and of themselves. They just are. They're neutral. The judgments and meanings you have of them are created by *you*. As illustrated in the tennis example, a situation can be interpreted in more than one way because people create their assessments based on their own maps of the world and their own unique programming.

As much as it seems like they do, circumstances, people, and events do NOT cause us to experience anything. It's your inner story about them that creates how you feel. The meaning or interpretations you give to what is before you is what you will react to, and what determines how you will respond emotionally and behaviorally moving forward. I invite you to read this paragraph at least a second time, and let it really sink in; because this is SO powerful.

Learning these key distinctions opens up new possibilities for you. You get to create more desirable experiences by choosing what story you tell and what new responses you want to experience. **You are a creator!**

Here are the key distinctions:

- **Reality/Assertions/Facts:** what's actually going on; the facts you can see *without* any extra meaning, interpretation, or judgment placed on them.

- **Interpretations/Assessments/Judgments:** The meaning you are giving the reality, or the story you are telling about it *as if it is true*. X means Y.

- **Feeling/Emotional response:** The feeling or emotion you have *in response* to the meaning/story you are holding as true. This can create positive or negative experiences/emotions. When we have negative assessments and interpretations, it often creates what we call inner "dramas". Remember, a feeling that doesn't feel good is also your emotional guidance, reminding you that you are not interpreting the situation as Spirit does.

Let's try some examples to first demonstrate our automatic tendency to create meaning.

What does it mean when someone's arms are folded over their chest?
What does it mean when someone brings you flowers?
What does it mean when someone's house is messy?
What does it mean when a person doesn't feel like talking?

If we asked five people these questions, we might get five different answers. Right? So, a more appropriate way for me to have asked you these questions would have been "What does it mean *to you* when..." However, can you see how we have a tendency to attach meanings as if they are THE meaning that everyone has, and that it's the truth, it's reality, it's "what is"?

I am not in any way suggesting that we stop giving meaning to or interpreting things. We need to do this to make sense of the world and to be able to act. But doing so with this new awareness of the difference between what's true and what's your interpretation will allow you to no longer be at the effect of your outer world, and to be able to choose how you feel. And, when you can choose how you think and feel, you are also choosing your vibration and your ability to manifest what you desire! You'll also have a lot fewer arguments!

Here are some examples of how you create how you feel, rather than the outer circumstances and facts causing your reactions.

Fact: Winter is coming.
Personal interpretation/inner story and meaning: It's going to be miserable.
Emotional response to this story: depressed

Someone else's interpretation of winter coming might be very different! To them, winter might mean time for fun winter sports, cozy nights by a fire, time to work on projects without distractions, and so on. Their emotional response might be eager anticipation!

Fact: Person –x– didn't offer to help.
Personal interpretation/inner story and meaning: S/he is selfish and doesn't care about me.
Emotional response to this story: Anger or resentment

Someone else's interpretation might be, "They must have some reason that's valid for them for not offering, even if I don't know what it is. I won't take it personally. Maybe they're tired. Maybe they're not comfortable with how to help or confident that they would do it right." Their emotional response would be peaceful acceptance, or they might just be curious and ask.

Fact: My date/friend didn't call me.
Personal interpretation/inner story and meaning: S/he must not like me. No one does.
Emotional response to this story: feeling insecure about whether you're likable, lovable, worthy, etc.

Someone else might not interpret this at all, and just be curious, wondering why they didn't call without taking it personally. They might not have any emotional response, other than feeling motivated to call and ask!

Are you starting to relate to this phenomenon?

Note: In some contexts, making assessments is necessary and valid. However, to be useful and effective, you want to be clear on the criteria being used for making the assessment. These standards can be just yours, if that's appropriate for the context, or they can be shared and agreed upon with others. For example, when hiring someone to do a job, you would have qualifications as your criteria. Societies also have shared standards, and one society's standards can be very different than others. Understanding this dynamic can help us to understand other people's choices and behaviors.

The "Is it True?" process (The one question that will set you free)

Here are a couple of exercises to help you learn how to apply this throughout your day. All of this is an integration of what I learned from my Ontological Design training with Dr. Fernando Flores, and from a similar process taught by the late Morty Lefkoe. Byron

Katie also teaches a similar process; and there are very likely others, as well, because these are very useful distinctions to be aware of. The main purpose is to raise awareness of when you're adding your own meanings and interpretations to events, and the effect that has on you.

Both your emotions and your body will let you know when you need to check within and ask if what you're thinking is actually true. Any undesirable feelings are a signal to check; and any physical discomfort or tension can be an indicator, too, since your body will always respond to your thoughts as if they are true.

It's important to become competent at settling your body down with calming, centering breathing, which you'll do in step #4. This allows you to observe or reflect on the interpretations you're making, and to override your automatic programs and triggered reactions. When you can do this, then you have choice.

Is it true exercises

To develop some competency with this process, I suggest practicing it for a few days. This way you won't be trying to learn it while you're already upset about something, and it will be easier to get the hang of it.

Exercise #1

1. Think of a negative reaction or emotion you had recently. (such as an angry, annoyed, or impatient reaction, or feeling bad about yourself)
2. What were the actual observable facts in the situation?
3. What meaning did you give it? *Make sure you get down deep enough to what's causing the feeling. It's not always the first interpretation that shows up. You might need to ask again, "What about this is making me feel bad?"*

4. *Breathe, relax, and center.* Shift to perplexity (a sense of open curiosity), and maybe even wonder.
   - Ask yourself, "Is this really "true", or just my interpretation?
   - What is my emotional guidance telling me?
5. How would you rather feel? What other interpretations are possible that would support this feeling?
   Tips:
   - Considering positive intentions can be very helpful.
   - Re-Source (expand to your whole Source/Spirit Self) and *consider your greater Spirit perspective.*
   - Consider how someone else, like a role model or friend, might interpret it.
   - If you were a lawyer in court, how might you argue *against* this interpretation and argue *for* a different one? What evidence is there to the contrary?
   - Consider how your future, older, wiser self who has overcome these types of situations and responses might interpret it.
6. How do you feel now with the new interpretations? What has opened up for you?

Here's another way you can practice:

Exercise #2

Set a schedule, for example, every hour for 5 hours, for which you will just stop and notice the following:

1. **What's the reality in front of me?** Examples: My boss is speaking to me. She is telling me she needs me to re-do my report.

2. **What meaning am I giving to this?** Example: My boss must be upset with me. I didn't do a good enough job. I'll never get it right. This is going to mess up everything. Or, this is just feedback. I'm glad we can openly partner on this.

3. **What feeling/emotion is being generated by my interpretation in #2?** Example: worry and anxiety; or confidence or ambition
   If it's not a positive feeling, continue:

4. **How do I *want* to feel? What other interpretations are possible that would support this feeling?** Examples: More relaxed, secure, and open. Maybe we just need to get clearer about the standards and what she needs. I just need to gather more information.

How and when to use the "Is it true?" process in the moment throughout your day

It's quite simple, really. *Whenever you don't feel good emotionally or physically, check in with your thinking:*

- "What am I thinking that's creating these feelings? How am I interpreting or attaching meaning to the facts before me that has me feeling this way?"

- *Breathe, relax, and center.* Shift to perplexity (a sense of open curiosity), and maybe even wonder.

- Ask yourself, "Is this really "true", or just my interpretation? (This is the "one question that will set you free".)

- What is my emotional guidance telling me?

- How would I rather feel? What other interpretations are possible that would support this feeling?

Tips:

- Considering positive intentions can be very helpful.

- Re-Source (expand to your whole Source/Spirit Self) and *consider your greater Spirit perspective.*

- Consider how someone else, like a role model, might interpret it.

- If you were a lawyer in court, how might you argue against this interpretation and argue for a different one? What evidence is there to the contrary?

- Consider how your future, older, wiser self who has overcome these types of situations and responses might interpret it.

Using the "Is it true?" process, and asking yourself, "Is this true, or just my interpretation?", can be one of the most empowering, freeing things you can do for yourself; and will allow you to be the happy, deliberate creator that you're meant to be!

Recap and practice

"Abracadabra! I create as I speak!" - your language doorway to the creative Soul that you are.

Since you create as you speak, which includes your thoughts, it's important to be aware of the language you use and to be mindful of your thinking and interpretations. When you want something, be sure to use language that creates an image of what you DO want versus what you don't want.

Setting intentions to deliberately create how you want to be and what you'd like to accomplish during your day can be truly magical, and fun! I hope you'll play with it.

Your thoughts will determine the quality of your present and future experiences. We live in our interpretations; so, if you have an undesirable emotion, check your interpretation! *YOU are creating how you feel. Emotions don't just happen to you.* The "Is it true" process is your way of managing this.

This week, my recommendations are:

- Practice the "Is it True process" with either exercise #1 or #2 at *least* once/day. Exercise #2 can be done in any moment, and only takes a few moments.

- Write your own morning intentions to use, and take notice at the end of the day how much of it came true.

- Set your intention to use outcome-oriented language, and to be mindful of when you and others are using problem-oriented language. You can even notice these patterns in movies and TV shows!

- Listen to the guided meditations below to support you in this learning. I think you're going to enjoy them.

At this time, I recommend listening to a 15 minute guided meditation called **"I am the space for"**. I love this simple way of meditating and have found it to be magically effective. It's just another form of setting your intentions, and reminds you that you are the space of pure potential, and you get to direct the form that potential will take. What do you want to be the space for? Love? Joy? Good times with friends? *Imagine and feel it as you say it, and "Abracadabra! It is done!"*.

The "Getting a different perspective" guided meditation.

Beliefs are also just interpretations that we hold as true. In this meditation, you'll begin with an issue that is problematic for you and you feel stuck about, becoming aware of the interpretations and beliefs embedded within your inner story about the issue. You'll be stepping into the minds of other people and role models that have a different, more useful perspective than yours, and then stating "I'm open to doubting...; and I'm more open to believing...". By doing this, you'll have the chance to experience that your way of thinking about something isn't the only way, and not necessarily true; and you'll start exercising your ability to shift your interpretations and beliefs!

To listen to the guided meditation recordings of "I am the Space for" or "Getting a different perspective", go to www.newpossibilitiescoaching .com/three-doorways-to-the-soul-book.html

CHAPTER SIX

Your Doorway of Emotions

- How to tell a better-feeling story to shift your emotions, vibration, and what you'll create
- Heart coherence for receiving guidance and wisdom from your Soul and to shift how you feel

As I mentioned earlier in the book, our language, body, and emotions are inseparable. Our bodies and emotions respond to the inner stories we tell ourselves and how we're interpreting what's going on. We become our stories; and we create with them, as well. And, they affect our vibration and, thus, influence what we manifest. Your stories either allow what you want to manifest, or close it down.

What do I mean by "stories"? Simply, they're your inner dialogue, or what you're saying to yourself in your thoughts. Of course, you can also speak them out loud. Here's an example: "I'm never going to have enough money to live the way I want to. I'll never qualify for a job that pays enough." or "I hate my boss! They don't know what they're doing and it makes work so much harder and miserable." We are living in our stories, both good feeling and bad feeling ones, all day. And, as I discussed earlier, sometimes we're talking about facts; but most of the time, we're interpreting what's before us.

Your emotions are the doorway through which your Soul communicates to you whether your stories are aligned with its greater perspective, or not. Like rumble strips on the highway that let you know when you're out of your lane, your unpleasing emotions alert you that you're temporarily disconnected from your Greater Spirit-Self. It's like that little sound on your GPS that signals you to correct when you're going the wrong way.

If you change your story to match the perspective of Spirit, you'll feel better; and, you'll be back on track towards your desires, as well! In this part of the book, I want to give you more strategies for how to change your stories that don't feel good to ones that feel better and *are also believable*. By doing so, you'll have more choice about what you can create, and about how you feel, rather than being at the effect of how your emotions seem to just happen to you and are not within your control.

Do not bypass your feelings. Listen to them.

There seems to be a lot of confusion as people learn about this approach to spirituality, in that many people think that since it's important to be positive and happy to manifest what you want, that you should bypass your feelings and "fake it 'til you make it", or deny your feelings and the problem and only focus on the positive. Perhaps this works for some folks, but it's not my recommendation. Your feelings are not a weakness. They are part of God's design for communicating with you! What a gift! Are you going to ignore or bypass that?

Your "negative" feelings are being generated by your inner narrative. If you try to change it inauthentically, it might feel good for a bit; but it's likely to find its way back, like a rubber band snapping back. I'm sure you've experienced this before.

Instead, like in the "Is it true?" process, I recommend listening to the stories to reveal that they are only your interpretations, not necessarily the truth; and that they are not Spirit's perspective. From there, you can find your way to change the story in a way *that is believable to you*, so it will stick, and so it won't be sending out "mixed signals" to the Universe.

I find it easiest and most empowering to incorporate appropriate Spirit presuppositions into the new story. Those are the new stories ready and available to you once you embody them. Here are some wording ideas to work your way towards that.

Also, as I've mentioned, I think it's really important to be fully congruent with your affirmations and stories; meaning, you want to fully believe what you're saying. Anything wobbly could just potentially end up creating more of what you don't want, like not being quite tuned into a radio station and hearing poor-quality sound.

Tips for how to talk about what you want and telling your new believable story

A good first tip is to ask yourself, "What do I *already* believe that I can apply to the situation, that will help me feel better or good about it?" Here's an example using some presuppositions of Spirit: "Even tho' I don't know how this is going to happen, or for certain, I trust and believe that Spirit/the Universe has a way, and is orchestrating the essence of what I want."

You don't need to figure out the hows that will make your story come true. That's not your job. Spirit will take care of that; and if you're tuned to the right frequency of Spirit, it will lead you to any hows that you need to act on. As for your story, you only need to speak in a way that creates an opening for it to happen, rather than shutting it down.

Some law of attraction teachings suggest thinking and talking about your desire in the present tense, as if it's already done. ("I'm rich! I have the vacation home I desire and love doing whatever I feel like every day!") If this feels believable to you, great! But if there's a part of you inside going "Not really!", try talking about it being *in process*. ("I love knowing that my desire is already created in my virtual reality and that I'm in the process of allowing it into my physical reality. I love knowing that I can get better and better at this.")

Here are some phrases you can adapt and use to make it even easier to hold your belief and positive feelings as you build your new outcome-oriented story. This list is not all-inclusive. Anything similar in nature that works for you will do!

I am in the process of…

I'm getting better and better at…

I love knowing that … (e.g., the Universe has already created what I've asked for, and all I have to do is allow it.)

I love knowing that I am the Space for…(pure potential, infinite possibilities, etc.)

I'm learning…

I wonder…

I'm open and willing to…, or I'm open to….., or "I'm open to receiving…"

I'm ready and eager for…

Perhaps …

I've decided…

It excites me… or I'm excited about, or I'm excited at the thought of…

I love the idea of…

It's going to be so great when…

I love it when…

I love seeing myself…

I can't wait for…

I can feel how close –x- is, and it feels so good!, or I'm getting closer and closer to…

What if …

It's possible that….

I wonder how it *could* be possible?

A fun little trick, of sorts, is to use 3rd person, using your name, instead of "I" in your story. (Ann is thinking/feeling….). It helps separate you from the issue and be more of an observer, or witness to it, making it easier to shift the story.

★★★★ *Is this really true, or just my interpretations? What else is possible? What evidence to the contrary exists?*

I was working with a client about various challenges she was experiencing that week, one of which was dealing with an extremely anxious rescue dog she had just adopted. She was saying things like, "This is going to be a lot of work. We've got a long road ahead of us. I'm trying everything, and it's not working." Of course, these thoughts did not feel good, nor were they helpful in allowing the solutions she needed to show up. They were focused on the problem, and keeping it there, with hard work all the way.

Instead, I suggested something like, "I'm open to how this can get better and how this can be easier. I'm sure the solutions I need exist and that what we want is possible. I'll just take one easy step at a time, and be open to guidance and delightful surprises along the way."

That felt much better! Can you feel how much more opening that is? It doesn't ignore the problem. It invites in and allows solutions for it which she will act on.

Here's another example:

Current story that doesn't feel good: My business is going so slowly. I just don't know what to do differently.

Some new stories/new ways of thinking about it: Even though I don't know yet what to do differently, I know the answers exist and are available to me. I'm open and willing for them to show up, and I invite them in. I love knowing that what I want is already done in my virtual reality. This is about more than just succeeding in my business. This is about learning how to allow in what I want and letting go of how I hold myself back. I'm excited to have these breakthroughs and this kind of growth. I wonder how I can open up those possibilities. I'm sure that many successful business people went through these stages. It's all just feedback, not failure. I wonder what else IS possible for me, since I am a creator and I create from infinite potential!

Did you pick up on how I incorporated some presuppositions of Spirit? And didn't it feel better?

Another approach is to begin by going more general about your negative thoughts. Then move to more general positives; then move to more specific positives

Often, when we're in a negative frame of mind and not feeling as we'd like, we're focused on specifics about a negative scenario or negative possibilities. For example: "I hate the project I'm working on at work and Joe is driving me crazy with his incompetence." (Then you'd start thinking in detail about all those things.)

When you do this, you're building up the drama of something you don't want, right? So you want to tell a new story. Yet, sometimes, it's too difficult to jump right into thinking about specifics for a positive story. It might be too big a jump.

So work your way into it gradually. Begin by going more general about your negatives. Then move to more general positives; then move to more specific positives. (or, at the least, stay in the general positives; as long as it leaves you feeling good).

Example continued from above: "Work isn't quite as I'd like it sometimes, and sometimes I get annoyed by certain people. At least it's just sometimes. I could put my focus on the positive aspects, and I could take responsibility for how I create my experience. I wonder how I could look at this differently. Perhaps I could begin to explore ways to make the project more meaningful or at least easier. How is this project important to what I do care about? (then add some specifics)

And how could I see Joe through my Source eyes? Of course, he's doing the best he can. Perhaps if I'm less resistant about this, and more open and allowing, a new way to handle this will unfold. I like believing that anything is possible and that I can bring joy to whatever I do and wherever I am."

Let's start pulling together the various strategies we've covered in the book. Pick one of your typical unhappy stories, and play around with some of these tips. I know that you'll feel the loosening and opening up that will occur. It's okay to be a beginner at learning this. You'll get better and better the more you play with it all.

1. Write your current story that doesn't feel good here:

2. *Breathe, center, and relax, even "Re-Source", if possible.*

3. Is this really true, or just my interpretations? What other interpretations are possible? What evidence to the contrary exists?

4. Some presuppositions of Spirit that could apply and I could incorporate into my new story (feel free to look at the list!):

5. "I'm open and willing to (fill in the blank)":

6. New story/new ways of thinking about it (use any of the tips listed):

Of course, and very importantly, always, always breathe, relax and center first before trying to tell your new story so that you'll shift out of that reactive state and have your resourceful brain available for you.

It's very powerful to relax by returning to your Whole Spirit-Self. You might be able to do this through meditation, or through your way of "Re-Sourcing" that you created with my meditations for that (Connecting to the Space of Stillness and Quiet, and the Box into Spirit meditations), or through centered breathing. Or, you might do it by going out in nature, or stroking your pet! If you play around with the various strategies in this book, you'll find your own way for returning to your Wholeness.

However, there are times when doing this is just too big a leap. You just can't feel Spirit, and your stories seem unchangeable because your body has been triggered into the survival mode we talked about. And, sometimes there's an underlying positive intention, like a part of us that just wants to be right, or just wants to feel what we're feeling and be allowed to do so. In times like this, you'll need to take extra steps to shift out of survival mode, to relax, and to shift your thinking. One strategy is creating heart coherence and connecting to your heart for guidance. Another, that I really love, is the Emotional Freedom Technique, also referred to as EFT or tapping. It's called emotional freedom because it frees you from unwanted emotions, and gives you freedom and choice over how you feel, rather than being at the effect of them.

Heart Coherence

Connecting to your inner wisdom and solution consciousness with heart coherence and the Heart Math process

As I've mentioned, we cannot panic our way to a solution, or to experiencing what we desire. When we panic, or stress over anything, our brain goes into fight or flight survival mode. When this happens, the higher functioning parts of the brain become limited in functioning, as all resources are directed to use of the part of the brain that impacts our ability to survive in actual physical life or death situations.

Day to day, even though our life is not actually in danger, our worrying and fearful thoughts about anticipating something undesirable and that we won't be okay in some way, trigger this survival part of the brain. This, in turn, has a huge ripple effect of physiological consequences, as well.

Since 1991, the Heart Math Institute (www.heartmath.org) has been researching and studying the intelligence and capabilities of the heart.

From their website:

> "New scientific research shows the human heart is much more than an efficient pump that sustains life. *The research suggests the heart also is an access point to a source of wisdom and intelligence that we can call upon to live our lives with more balance, greater creativity and*

enhanced intuitive capacities. All of these are important for increasing personal effectiveness, improving health and relationships, and achieving greater fulfillment."

"The heart is, in fact, a highly complex information-processing center with its own functional brain, commonly called the heart brain, that communicates with and influences the cranial brain via the nervous system, hormonal system and other pathways. These influences affect brain function and most of the body's major organs and play an important role in mental and emotional experience and the quality of our lives."

When you're in a "heart coherent" state, you are connected to the intelligence of your heart, which is connected to the field of Spirit, as well as your brain. They are working together in balance. Numerous studies have shown that heart coherence is an optimal physiological state associated with increased cognitive function, self-regulatory capacity, emotional stability, and resilience. It improves your level of performance, your health, and your level of happiness. It also activates your innate ability to heal.

Some ways to achieve heart coherence are:

- Relax your mind and body, as you do in meditation and thru proper breathing.

- Think of calming, positive thoughts, memories, or images

- You can also achieve heart coherence through gratitude, or focusing on what's good and right in your world, and what you have to appreciate (as opposed to our tendencies to notice and focus on what is or could go wrong).

- Connect to a sense of peace and stillness, even just in the space around you. It is always available to you! One of my favorite ways is fully recalling how I feel when my cat is purring on my lap. So easy.

Heart Math from chaos to coherence process and meditation

Use this process to release unwanted thoughts (stories) or feelings, or if you're just feeling off-centered in some way. It will help you to connect to the inner guidance and wisdom of your heart, and return to your more peaceful, resourceful Spirit-Self. The recording of me guiding you through this is available, as well.

1. Bring to mind something you'd like to release. Some possibilities are uncomfortable feelings, thoughts or stories, a limiting mindset or emotion, or some tension in the body; a situation in your life that's making you feel worried, anxious, impatient, frustrated, hopeless, etc.

2. As you think about your issue, become aware of how you feel. Just notice your feelings, and maybe even label them, such as sad, or anxious, or frustrated, etc. Rate it from 1- 10, 10 being the most intense.

3. It's all right that you've been thinking and reacting as you have. You've been doing the best you knew how and were able to.
Let yourself become objective about the issue at hand by imagining this as someone else's problem, and seeing it more from a distance or a bird's eye view, and leave the problem or issue *out there*.

4. Close your eyes and get comfortable.

5. Feel your body as a whole from the inside, focusing on the space- the space within, and the space it occupies. Scientists claim that the body is more space than matter. Imagine and feel your inner body as open, clear, spacious awareness.

6. Breathe into this space. As you inhale, imagine gradually and completely filling the space of your body with your breath; and

as you exhale, imagine emptying it completely. Take several of these slow, deep breaths.

7. Now shift your focus to the area around your heart, and take 4 or 5 slow, full breaths; and allow yourself to relax the best you can. Perhaps you can imagine your heart area opening and expanding with each breath.

8. Recall a very positive memory or think about something really positive for you. Let yourself re-experience it as fully as you can so you can feel it again now; so that you even feel a small smile on your face. (Appreciation, gratitude, love...)

Let those smiling, positive feelings spread into the space of your body with your breaths, into every crevice and space of your being, filling with the positive feelings/with the smile.

If your attention wanders, gently return it to your heart area, breathe and relax some more, and you can simply return to the positive memories and feelings, to let go of control; and you can just allow the good feeling states from your heart naturally arise within you.

Rest in your heart and the positive thoughts and feelings that arise. *This is your connection to your inner being and greater Spirit-Self.*

Soak and relax any disturbing or perplexing feelings from your original issue in the love, compassion, and wisdom of your open heart, like soaking something in the sink. Just let love and compassion soak them up, and, a little at a time, let it dissolve the significance and meaning you've been attaching to it; remembering that it's never the problem or issue itself that causes discomfort and energy drain, as much as the meaning you assign to it.

When you let any resistance and difficulties soak in the love, compassion, and wisdom of your heart, how does it change?

9. Now, from deep in your heart and *its connection to Spirit*, ask for appropriate guidance or insight.
   Ask your heart any or all of these options:

   - "What would be a more efficient and effective response to this situation, that would minimize my stress now and in the future?"

   - "What are some other ways I can achieve my positive intention without the negative consequences?"

   - "What's most important to me, right here and now?"

   - "What do you want me to know or remember?"

   - "How else could I interpret or think about this?"

   - "What else is possible? How can this be better/easier?"

   Sometimes this comes in a flash, sometimes softly and subtly, sometimes over time. *You don't need to focus on getting the answer. Just go back to staying in your heart space by holding your positive thoughts, or just being in stillness and quiet. While you do that, intuitive clarity can show up.* Whether you get a specific response now or later doesn't matter as much as that you've taken some time to connect with the essence of who you are.

Just linger for a while in the heart, focusing on appreciation, or love, or whatever it guides you to.

1. When you do get a message from your heart, ask some part of you to be responsible for generating these new possibilities in the future, thank it for doing so; and fully imagine this future.

2. When you feel ready, gently bring yourself back to write about your insights, taking whatever glimmers of peace, or release, or insight you gained, while continuing to hold the positive feelings generated by your heart.

3. In doing this, I shifted from _____ (head response) to _____ (intuitive heart response).

4. Now reflect back to what that unwanted feeling or tension was that you had at the start of the meditation. Now, on a scale of 1-10, how would you rate it?

This will also create changes at the neuro-electrical and biochemical levels! And, best of all, you will feel so much better.

Keep in mind, the guidance may show up gradually, especially if it's a big issue you were addressing. If you didn't get a clear shift or answers on the spot, continue to focus on what there is to appreciate, as it can keep you from being pulled back into undesirable patterns, and eventually bring you more clarity. You might even just continue with your day; and, having settled yourself, the guidance will subtly show up at some point.

To listen to my guided meditation recording of this "From Chaos to Heart Coherence" process, go to www.newpossibilities coaching.com/three-doorways-to-the-soul-book.html.

Recap and practice

From Abraham, collective consciousness of Spirit, channeled by Esther Hicks:

> *"If you will let your dominant intention be to revise and improve the content of the stories you tell every day of your life, it is our absolute promise to you that your life will become those ever-improving stories.*

> *For by the powerful Law of Attraction—the essence of that which is like unto itself is drawn—it must be!"*
>
> *Excerpted from Money and the Law of Attraction on 8/31/08*

Now if that isn't motivation to attend to your stories, I don't know what is.

Abraham has also said,

> "If you thought a negative thought and a brick would instantly fall on your head every time, you'd clean up your thinking. But you're not here to be punished for your thinking. You're here to use your thinking, and your focus, to create."

So, here's my invitation to you. Moment to moment, notice how you feel; and if it isn't good, don't put up with it! This is being mindful.

1st Ask yourself, WHAT STORY AM I TELLING MYSELF that's creating my current feelings?

2nd Breathe, relax, and center; and let yourself be in a mood of perplexity. Just be openly curious!

3rd Then, to help you create a new, better-feeling story, consider these:

- Challenge the assessments embedded in your story. Are they really true? ("Is it true?" process) What other interpretations are possible? If you were a lawyer in court, how might you argue against this assessment and argue for a different one? What evidence is there to the contrary?

- Are there other people's perspectives that might be helpful to remember and apply to the situation?

- Could you ask, "Who am I being?" and "Re-Source"/reconnect to the space of stillness, quiet, and Spirit to get your greater Source/Spirit-Self perspective?

- Or could you connect to your heart space – one of LOVE, and ask what would be a more useful response/story for this situation?

- Maybe there's a part of you that has a positive intention that you need to take care of in a new way.

- If you still feel too stuck, use EFT/tapping to release and shift, which we'll talk about next.

With a commitment to doing this, you'll soon be able to use this process and approach in just minutes, or even less!

Everything in this book can be used to help you tell a better-feeling story! It's all about relaxing and opening up to thinking in new ways, from a higher vibrational perspective ("Re-Sourcing"). *Then, once you change, the world around you will change, too.*

Setting your vibrational momentum for the day before you start your day, like with morning intentions and meditation, is a great practice. It will help you to be more likely to tell good feeling stories in the first place!

Be easy with yourselves, and have fun with this!

Guided meditation practice:

Here's a beautiful guided meditation for changing your inner story from inside the vortex of love, which is the same as returning to your whole Spirit-Self. When you're in the space of Spirit, you more naturally create your story from Spirit perspectives.

To listen to the "Changing your story from inside the vortex of love and Spirit's perspective" guided meditation, go to www.newpossibilitiescoaching.com/three-doorways-to-the-soul-book.html.

CHAPTER SEVEN

Using all Three Doorways of your Soul With the Emotional Freedom Technique/Tapping

- The Emotional Freedom technique, also called tapping or EFT, to shift your stories and the triggered emotions of your reactive, survival mode

- Using EFT to shift from small self stories and feelings, back to the perspective of Spirit, to return to your greater Self

- Using EFT to shift limiting, small-self beliefs to the unlimited presuppositions of your Spirit-Self

Tapping is like having magic in your fingertips! It works similarly to acupuncture, in that you tap on energetic meridian points on your body to help deactivate the fight or flight survival/stress response, and to stimulate a relaxation response instead. Tapping without even saying anything can still have a very powerful, relaxing effect. You can use it just for relaxing, to help you shift into meditation, to help you go to sleep; and, by adding speaking, to help you shift your inner narratives and thus your emotions and your vibration. Since it releases stress, and thus lowers all the stress hormones that surge through you, it's also very healthy for your body and activates your body's innate abilities to heal. So, there are multiple reasons to give this a try! Here, we're going to focus on using it to shift your inner story and emotional state.

Have you ever tried to talk yourself out of a bad feeling while still feeling it? It doesn't often work too well, does it? Instead, what you'll find as you tap, is that as the tapping helps you to release the fight or flight response and to begin to relax, you're able to more easily shift your inner narrative. And, because it's also engaging your body and neurology, it seems to help get the new story more embodied, so it will be more likely to stick. It's almost like updating a software program that has a bug. *You'll be tapping into your energetic body and neurology, using language, and shifting emotions – using all three doorways to your Soul!*

Tapping is a very organic process that allows an easy revealing of deeper layers of stories and beliefs that need to be uncovered for real change. When done properly, a very deep, cathartic release *naturally* happens, and then you're able to transition to a more positive perspective.

This is a different approach than traditional "positive thinking." You're not being dishonest with yourself. You're not trying to obscure the stress and anxiety inside yourself with a veneer of insincere affirmations. Rather, you lovingly confront and deal with the anxiety and negative feelings, offering deep and complete acceptance to both your feelings and yourself. Then, you're authentically able to turn your thoughts and vibrations to the powerful and positive. That's what makes EFT so much more effective than the "positive thinking" techniques that you may have already tried. It's not just a mental trick. Instead, you'll be using positive phrases and EFT tapping to tune into the very real energy of positivity, affirmation, and joy that is natural and implicit inside you. You're changing your body's energy into a more positive flow, a more positive vibration, and… returning to the true you.

How a basic EFT sequence works:

- Identify the emotion or issue you want to focus on. It can be general anxiety, or it can be a specific emotion, thought, belief, situation, or issue which causes you to feel "bad", and thus creates resistance to allowing what you want.

- Think about the situation creating your negative/resistant state. How do you feel about it right now? Allow yourself to get into and *really feel the emotion*, as this is very important to the process working for you. Talking about it can be useful to help you really feel it. Rate the intensity level of it, with zero being the lowest level of intensity and ten being the highest.

- Compose your setup statement. Your setup statement should acknowledge the problem or emotion you want to deal with, then follow it with an unconditional affirmation of yourself as a person. (More on this below)

- Follow the tapping sequence below until you feel relief. As you tap on each point, let your automatic thoughts flow, letting the small self "speak" to raise your awareness of it and its narrative. Eventually, you'll feel a natural, organic letting go and readiness to begin shifting to a more positive, useful story. *Don't force it before you feel the readiness.* Continue tapping, repeating the cycle of points as many times as necessary.

- Tap on one point per sentence/phrase, or a collection of related thoughts.

- There's no one or right way to do this. It can be different every time! I've found that even if you miss points or tap on not exactly the right point, it still works beautifully. In fact, there are several variations of tapping out there, some very lengthy. I like the simplicity of this version.

Here are the steps with more detail, followed with a link to a demo video:

1. Begin with creating a setup statement: "Even though –x–, I love and accept myself." or "I'm willing to love and accept myself as best I can." Examples:

   "Even though I feel this anxiety, I love and accept myself."

   "Even though I'm anxious about my interview, I deeply and completely accept and love myself.

   "Even though I'm feeling this anxiety about my financial situation, I honor these feelings, and deeply and completely accept and love myself."

   "Even though I panic when I think about _____, I love and accept myself as best I can."

   "Even though I'm worried about how to approach my boss, I deeply and completely accept and love myself."

   "Even though I'm having trouble breathing, I deeply and completely accept and love myself."

2. Perform the setup: With four fingers on one hand, tap the Karate Chop point on your other hand. The Karate Chop point is along the outer edge of the hand, like the part of your hand you would hit a board with using a karate chop.

   While feeling the feelings, repeat the setup statement three times aloud, while simultaneously tapping the Karate Chop point. You can vary what you say for your 2nd and 3rd setup statements. Now take a deep breath.

3. Begin tapping on the rest of the points. As you tap on each point in the diagram, you can simply repeat a simple *reminder phrase*, such as "my anxiety" or "my interview" or "my financial situation." Or, you can simply freely associate, speaking whatever thoughts come to

mind, like venting to a friend. I find this second approach much more powerful, as it reveals the story you want to change and eventually has you create a new one.

Sometimes we have feelings and don't even know why! It happens when we're not aware of the inner narratives we're having. If this is the case, simply start with the feelings, and then just free associate and explore what starts to show up. So, as you begin, you might say something like, "Even tho' I'm feeling -x-, and I don't even know why, I love and accept myself as best I can, and let it be okay."; and then on to phrases something like this, one point at a time: "I'm feeling off somehow. I'm not even sure what I'm feeling. And I don't even know why. But something is bothering me. ", and so on. Trust me, the clarity will eventually come through.

Here are some tips to help you achieve the right tapping technique.

- You should use a firm but gentle pressure, as if you were drumming on the side of your desk. It's a tapping pressure similar to the reflex test a doctor does on your knee.

- You can use all four fingers, or just the first two (the index and middle fingers). Four fingers are generally used for the set-up, on the top of the head, the collarbone, under the arm... wider areas. On sensitive areas, like around the eyes, you can use just two.

- You can use one hand, tapping on the points on one side of the body. Or you can use two hands, tapping on the points on both sides of the body (where it will work).

- Tap with your fingertips, not your fingernails or the pads. The sound will be round and mellow.

- After the set up on the karate point, the tapping order begins at the inner eyebrow and works down; then ends by returning to the top of the head, to complete the loop.

- Tap *roughly* 5-7 times on each point in the following sequence:

For a short video of me demonstrating tapping, go to www.newpossibilitiescoaching.com/three-doorways-to-the-soul-book.html. Remember how I said that it's okay and that the process will still work, even if you miss a point or don't do it "perfectly"? Well, I actually missed the under-eye point a couple of times in the first demonstration! But, no worries! Right?

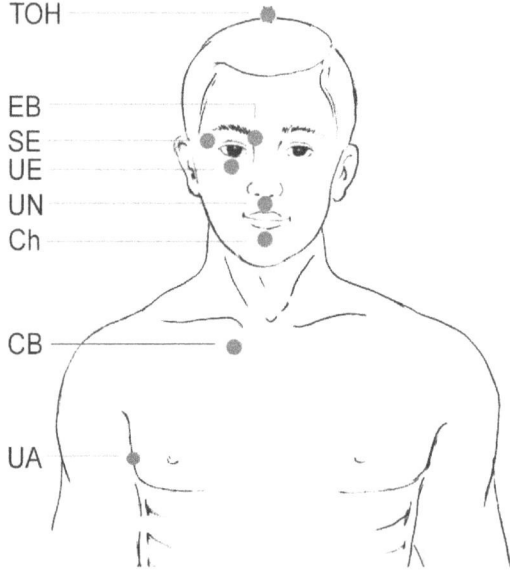

Eyebrow: The inner edges of the eyebrows, where the eyebrow begins. Use two fingers.

Side of eye: The bony, hard area *just outside the eye*. (not the temple) Use two fingers.

Under eye: The bony, hard area under the eye, that merges with the cheekbone, in line beneath the pupil. Use two fingers.

Under nose: The point centered between the bottom of the nose and the upper lip. Use two fingers.

Chin: This point follows symmetrically with the previous one, and is centered between the bottom of the lower lip and the chin.

Collarbone: Tap *just below* the hard ridge of your collarbone with four fingers.

Underarm: On your side, about four inches beneath the armpit. Use four fingers.

Head: The crown, center, and top of the head. Tap with all four fingers.

4. Continue tapping through as many rounds as you need. Allow what you're really feeling and want to say out of your system, without holding back. Swear, yell, cry, whatever! This will allow a much-needed, powerful release. Tapping is a very organic process when done right. You don't need to force or rush any of it. At some point, you'll feel a cathartic release, like a big sigh, and a shift in your thinking and how you feel. You'll begin to hear the lack of "facts" and truth in your story, and how it's only one way of interpreting. It might even start to sound ridiculous, once your small self gets out of the way and releases its hold on you. Many people even laugh at this point. Sometimes you might get teary or cry just as a release and relief. It's all good. Once you feel this natural releasing and readiness, then you can continue to the next step. Trying to jump too soon to a positive story might not feel genuine, and might not be as effective. I cannot emphasize this enough.

5. Once you feel your emotion loosening, you're ready to begin installing some positive ways of thinking about your issue, building in a new positive story as you continue through the tapping sequence, again doing as many rounds as needed. (more tips below)

6. Let yourself ease into a new positive story. If you were supporting a friend in considering a different way of thinking about an upsetting issue, you probably wouldn't jump right to a different perspective, like, "Don't worry! Everything's going to work out for you!" Right? You'd find a way to work towards that idea. I recommend you do this for yourself with your tapping statements, as well. Then, at some point, you'll naturally feel complete. To finish, take some nice full breaths. Notice how you feel, and rate it again on a scale of 1 -10. How does it compare to your original rating?

7. If you feel complete, you're done. You might feel complete enough for just now; and you can continue at another time, working through any remaining layers of the story, or additional stories, that still need to show up. The more you get at the details and roots of your issue, the better. If you don't, no worries. They'll likely show up again for you as another opportunity for releasing more "small-self" thinking, so you can experience your "greater, Spirit-Self" more and more.

Tips for wording

Here are some examples of positive affirmations you can use in your set-up statement, after the "Even though I (undesirable feeling, thoughts, belief, issue, etc.)". You can use as many as you like in each set-up statement! You can even ramble on!

"Even though I feel (or think) - x -...

- I choose to relax and accept myself now
- I love and accept myself, or, I love and accept myself as best I can
- I choose to forgive myself and feel good about myself
- I choose to release this now and love and accept myself as I am today
- I choose to release this -x- and feel relaxed and calm within
- I choose to remember that I'm only human and humans make mistakes/are all perfect in their imperfections
- I'm open to..(ex: seeing this a different way)
- I'm letting that go, and choosing...(ex: something that feels better)
- I'm choosing a new identity that honors all of who I am and can be
- I'd really like x, y, z and I invite that in
- I'm beginning to think...
- I'm open and willing to... (ex: how this can be better/easier, what else is possible)
- I honor these feelings as emotional guidance from my Soul/greater Spirit-Self/Spirit that I'm just not perceiving this situation as Spirit does
- I invite in...

To help you gradually shift to a new, believable story, here are some ideas for useful questions and statements to use during your tapping as you feel ready:

- I wonder how I might think about this differently.
- Letting it go, what if I could let this go?
- I wonder what it's about
- What are the messages or positive intentions behind this...? I choose to allow those messages now.
- I choose to relax in my body. And pay attention to what I feel. It's safe to relax in my body. It's safe to feel these feelings. It's safe to release... Letting it go.
- Who would I be without this -x-?
- What if I could (let it go, release this -x-)? What if I could (heal, be free of, forgive, etc.)

- It's exciting to think about. Just the possibility is exciting.
- It's safe/okay to let go of this -x-. It's safe to feel good again, and it's safe to feel good about what's possible.
- It feels good to do this.
- Maybe....(example: this can be easier than I thought)

I consider these next ones especially valuable to incorporate:

- This story I've been telling myself. Maybe it isn't "true". What other interpretations are possible? What would Spirit/Source say? or How does Spirit think about this?
- What evidence is there to the contrary of what I've been telling myself? (then proceed to tap in all the evidence, one tapping point per evidence)
- I am open to discovering/learning...
- I'm open to letting this be easy. (or fun, or whatever)
- How could this get better?
- What else is possible?

Using meditation music to assist you

Since part of what makes tapping work is the relaxing of your survival-based, smaller-self mind, I also find it helpful to play meditative music while tapping. I find it makes the process even more relaxing and even easier to go deep and have a profound impact.

With tapping and meditation, you are shifting your frequency, and tuning yourself to the field of potential, the creative space of Spirit. It's in this space that deeper, more lasting changes can transpire.

As I mentioned in the meditation tips, I like music specifically designed with frequencies for meditation, like Solfeggio frequency music. But any meditative music that does its magic for you will obviously do.

Using tapping to return to your Spirit-Self perspective

Tapping is generally used to release pain-inducing stories that you're holding and to shift to *any* better feeling story. I have found for myself and my clients that using tapping to return to your Whole Self by returning to your Spirit perspective is even more powerful. The tapping will help you relax the reactionary, limited, fearful, small, separate self you're stuck in, so you can then become more resourceful, including remembering who you really are and what you would presuppose about your issue as the eternal, magical, unlimited, loving Spirit that you really are.

This approach to tapping also helps you to further embody your greater perspective for the future. Everything in this book is aimed at helping you to live throughout your day more and more as your Spirit-Self and from that perspective. Consider tapping another way to build this competency.

Here are some examples of how this shift to Spirit perspective might go, once you've fully expressed how you feel and have felt a cathartic shift.

"I was doing the best I knew and was able to at the time." "I know there's a positive intention." "How does my Spirit-Self perceive this?"

"Maybe I don't need to know exactly (how to get there, how this makes sense, why this happens, etc.). I can just focus on the single step ahead of me. And trust that the answers will appear. Maybe I can even enjoy this process."

"It's okay not to know how this will happen. Uncertainty means infinite possibilities are available to me!"

All you're doing is revealing the stories, or perspectives, of your limited small-self perspective, and re-interpreting your issue with appropriate presuppositions held by Spirit. I find that this makes it even easier to find a new, positive story that feels good, and believable; and that it's *very* uplifting and empowering. I highly encourage you to try this approach!

Another strategy that often shows up as appropriate and helpful for me during tapping, is addressing the positive intention of the small self when it's exerting its power. Its underlying concern is usually to feel safe, or loved, or to feel good. So, I authentically thank it for that intention as I continue to tap, and lovingly let it know that its approach isn't accomplishing what it wants for me. It could even put me more at risk by restricting me so much and causing stress, etc. Then, as I relax and return to my Spirit perspective, the awareness arises that being my Whole Spirit-Self is the best way to take care of my underlying positive intention (such as to stay safe, or feel good, or whatever), as that's how I have my greatest creative power and access to all possibilities that match the essence of my desire (including staying safe)! Tada! You'll notice this strategy in the sample script provided here.

In sum, here's a nice, simple sequence to follow, to use tapping to shift to Spirit perspectives:

- As part of your setup statements, say something like, "I honor these feelings *as guidance*. I'm just being my small self, and I just need to return to my whole, Spirit-Self."

Proceed with the loosening of your current stories and feelings; and then, once you've felt a cathartic shift or readiness, begin asking questions like:

- Are my thoughts really true? Are they assertions/facts, or assessments?

- What's the positive intention or concern underlying this feeling?

- What would Source say about this? How might Spirit take care of this concern?

- What would my greater Spirit-Self perspective be about this?

Whatever you choose to say, make sure you're not forcing it, and it feels believable. You can refer to the tips for how to tell a new believable story in Part Six.

Sample tapping script for feelings of urgency, panic, anxiety or overwhelm

This sample EFT script adapted from a tapping meditation by The Tapping Solution (www.thetappingsolution.com), is designed to produce a shift from general feelings of urgency, overwhelm or panic. It's easy and can even be fun! As a script, it might look long; but it really only takes about 16 minutes. Remember, you can also play meditation music while doing this. I've also provided a recorded version you can follow along with.

With any tapping meditations you're following that are by someone else, if a statement isn't a match for you, just replace it with something of your own that feels more appropriate. Feel free to adapt for yourself in any way that feels right. Tapping meditations are merely meant to help you with the process, if needed.

- First, think about a situation for which you feel a sense of urgency, or overwhelm, or panic, or anxiety. Give it a number on a scale of 0 – 10, 10 being the most intense: _____

- Now, take three slow, deep, and full breaths.

- Now flow into and follow the sample tapping script below. Again, as you tap, feel free to change any lines to more appropriately match what you're thinking or feeling. *Be sure to feel the emotions as you express them.*

Three set-up statements:

Karate Chop: Even though I feel so much urgency and overwhelm, I honor these feelings, and deeply and completely accept myself.

Karate Chop: Even though I feel so much urgency and anxiety in my life right now, I honor these feelings as emotional guidance from my Soul, and I love and accept myself as best I can.

Karate Chop: Even though I feel so much urgency and panic around getting everything done and making progress in my life, I am just being my small-self right now, which is okay; but it's time to relax and return to my whole, Spirit-Self, and accept how I feel.

Do the rounds:

Inner eyebrow: I'm feeling so much urgency and anxiety

Side of Eye: I really need things to change or (state your fear of what might happen)

Under Eye: I really need my situation to transform fast or (state fear of what might happen)

Under Nose: I really need things to improve

Under Mouth/Chin: I can't go on like this

Collarbone area: It's been too long already

Under Arm: I feel so much overwhelm around this and need things to change now

Top of Head: It feels like I can't wait any longer

Inner eyebrow: I feel so much anxiety around all of this. I feel like I need to do something. I need to fix this. I need to figure it out.

Side of Eye: But I feel so stressed I don't know what to do.

Under Eye: And that makes me feel confused and powerless. I feel so powerless.

Under Nose: Like there's nothing I can do to change things

Under Mouth/Chin: I can feel so much urgency and anxiety around all of this

Collarbone area: It's really stressful

Under Arm: I don't know what's going on, but I know I have positive intentions behind these feelings. I wonder what they are. I guess I just want everything to be okay. I appreciate this intention.

Top of Head: This urgency and panic aren't helping me be okay. They're getting in the way. If I relax, I'll be more resourceful and effective. And that will help everything to be okay.

Inner eyebrow: Maybe I can begin to let myself open and relax into this process

Side of Eye: Maybe as I feel calmer, the best next step and solutions will show up for me.

Under Eye: I can make more progress when I'm more relaxed

Under Nose: Are these limiting thoughts true facts, or just my interpretation?

Under Mouth/Chin: I'm really just making these thoughts up. These thoughts are only one possibility.

Collarbone area: What would my higher Source-Self say about this?

Under Arm: As I allow myself to open and relax into this process, I open myself to the infinite possibilities that support the essence of what I desire.

Top of Head: The essence of what I desire is already created and done in the field of potential.

Inner eyebrow: As I relax and remember who I fully am, I allow that desire to manifest.

Side of Eye: I'm not really powerless. I'm only feeling that way. I am a creator. It feels good to remember my power and all that's possible through my thoughts and focus.

Under Eye: As I relax more and more, I can act more from guidance and inspiration instead of fear.

Under Nose: And still make progress. Maybe even more progress.

Under Mouth/Chin: It really is safe to relax

Collarbone area: And to trust this process

Under Arm: When I let go of fear, I have all that Spirit is and all that I am available to me. And that's much safer.

Top of Head: Being relaxed is much safer than being stressed by fears.

Inner eyebrow: I'm open to releasing this sense of urgency and panic now

Side of Eye: I'm open to letting go of any remaining urgency and anxiety now

Under Eye: I'm open to receiving new ways of thinking.

Under Nose: I'm open to receiving my next steps and solutions.

Under Mouth/Chin: I have so many resources available to help me.

Collarbone area: Including all the resources of the Universe!

Under Arm: I am feeling calmer, and more and more relaxed

Top of Head: All is well.

Now, take three slow, deep, and full breaths.

Notice how you feel and on a scale of 0 – 10, rate the intensity of your sense of urgency, panic or overwhelm now in this space here: _____

If still needed, or if another layer shows up, continue to tap until you feel a shift and get the relief you're seeking. Notice any insights or questions that may have arisen.

Did you notice the gradual shift to Spirit perspectives? Are there others that might also help you remember the power and possibilities that exist for you?

To listen to a guided meditation recording for tapping on feelings of urgency, panic, anxiety, or overwhelm, go to www.newpossibilitiescoaching.com/three-doorways-to-the-soul-book.html.

Using EFT/Tapping to shift a limiting belief

Just as a quick review, an assertion is a fact we can provide evidence for. ("It's snowing today.")

An assessment is a judgment or interpretation based on personal, and sometimes shared, standards. ("The weather is lousy today.") It's the meaning we attach to something.

What's a belief? A belief is just an assessment, or interpretation, that you made about something in the past, and *that you hold as true*, like a fact or "the" truth, *over time*. We could also call it a story that you hold as true over time.

As a possible example, if your parents put in a lot of hours at work and you often heard them talk about it, you might have formed a belief like, "It takes really hard work to make money." Someone else may not have made that connection or interpretation, and had the experience of "Money comes to me easily!"

Beliefs are a powerful influence in *every* aspect of your life. Both conscious and unconscious beliefs have equal ability to empower you or limit you from living the life you choose. Your beliefs engage more of your neurology than your behaviors and mental strategies, and, consequently, have *more* impact on your degree of effectiveness. You can be "doing" all the "right" things towards a goal, but if your beliefs are not in alignment with that goal, you will essentially be holding yourself back, and only struggling towards your goal. For example, you might want more love in your life; but if you don't believe that you deserve it, the energy for your goal is sort of "short-circuited", metaphorically speaking.

Most of your beliefs were formed during your childhood when you interpreted or gave meaning to a particular external event, or recurring events. You formed those judgments *from the limited capabilities and filters you had as a child,* yet they continue to influence you throughout your life. These beliefs will determine what actions you will or will not take, and how you react to things, as well.

For example, if you were praised for doing well in school, and for other behaviors, you might have interpreted that as meaning "I earn people's love and approval by what I do and doing a good job."

It doesn't mean that was true. Your parents likely loved you no matter what; but as a child, you weren't able to discern that. Then, because you held the interpretation over time, it became a belief even into your adult life.

Or, maybe, if you were scolded or yelled at for doing something wrong, you might have interpreted it as meaning that you wouldn't be loved if you made mistakes. Not necessarily true, of course. But, as a child, that's the meaning you attached to those behaviors, and it became a belief.

Remember, most of this is out of our conscious awareness!

In reflection, can you think of some possible examples from your own childhood and life?

Beliefs are also self-reinforcing. What we believe, we tend to notice; and it will show up as seeming evidence and keep reinforcing your belief. You might not even notice all the evidence to the contrary, so it *seems* like the truth. For example: "Massachusetts drivers are terrible drivers.", or "There are no good men.".

I remember a woman in her mid 30's who came to me because she was still single, and wanted a relationship with a man. As we spoke, I uncovered her belief that there were no good men "out there" and thus the situation was hopeless. We proceeded to find evidence to the contrary (For example: If there are NO good men out there, is every woman in a relationship with a "bad" man?). I also helped her to remember Spirit's perspective. (Of course there was a good man for her if she asked for one! She was merely not allowing him in.) She became open to the idea that her story was not a truth, but only a truth she was creating. It was a big ah-ha moment for her. Within a week or two, she was dating; and not much later, she was in a relationship!

Beliefs can be like knots. We often just need to loosen them first, by creating doubt by providing new evidence from which to draw a new conclusion, or becoming aware that other interpretations are also possible.

Sometimes, our beliefs will naturally change as we mature, or as we have new experiences and become aware of new evidence for a new belief. Few adults still believe in Santa Claus in the way they did as a child, for example. But many beliefs stick with us through time and can be very challenging to change.

Tapping is very effective for loosening and shifting undesirable beliefs. Your whole life, you have been like great lawyers arguing *for* your limiting beliefs. With tapping, you can start creating a new case *against* your limiting, problematic beliefs by finding evidence to the contrary and exploring other possible interpretations.

Here, with tapping, we're going to focus on revealing that the limiting belief is merely an interpretation of the small self, and then shift to the perspective, the beliefs actually, held by Spirit.

The process for shifting from small-self beliefs to beliefs held by Spirit

The tapping process for this is essentially the same as what we just covered, with the focus being on your beliefs, rather than just how you're feeling. First, you want to raise your awareness of what limiting beliefs you're holding as true. Sometimes they become self-evident when you're tapping on an emotion and the story creating it. Other times, you need to do a little detective-type work to uncover it. If so, here are the steps.

Step 1: If you don't already have a belief you're aware of, you can think of something you want or a goal you have that you're having trouble with manifesting. Only small-self beliefs hold you back from manifesting what you want. *Therefore, you can consider each unfulfilled desire as a gift, as it can reveal to you what those limiting beliefs are. It's another opportunity for expanding more into your whole Spirit-Self and experiencing life from that perspective.*

Rate the intensity of your feelings around your unfulfilled desire, from 1-10, with 10 being the most intense. *If you have a belief ready to shift, rate the intensity of feelings around it, then skip to step three.*

Step 2: When you think about what you want, but don't have, what are your automatic thoughts about it, other than feeling bad? What stories do you tell yourself about it? These will reveal the beliefs you're holding.

If needed, you can use any or all of the questions below to help reveal the limiting belief(s). The intention here is to draw out your inner narrative and the limiting belief(s) hidden in there.

- What are you thinking that's making you feel that way? What's your inner narrative/story about this? *"I feel this way because...."* For example…. "This makes me feel overwhelmed because part of me thinks this is impossible. I've never been able to do this before. Who am I to achieve this?" The belief embedded in this is, "It's not possible if I haven't done it before." and maybe "I'm not worthy/don't deserve this."

- What's stopping you from having what you want? (first things that come to mind) Example: "I'm not in a relationship because there are no good men out there."

- Talk about it in the "problem frame" to reveal your limited thinking: "This is a problem because….", or "This feels true because..." (your explanation/story about why you have this problem)

- "A fear I have about this is…" For example, "I'm afraid I'll never have enough money."

Note: If more than one limiting belief shows up, write them all down, and tap on each one separately.

Step 3: Begin the tapping process as noted before, with music, if you like.

- As part of your set up, remind yourself that "Even though I'm feeling -x-, or thinking -x- (like I'll never have enough money), I honor these uncomfortable thoughts (or feelings/emotions) *as guidance that I'm just being my small self; and I just need to return to my whole, Spirit-Self.*"

- Tap on the belief that came from the untrue interpretations and/or limited perspectives from your smaller self until you feel a readiness and openness to begin shifting. Take your time with it, really feeling each statement as you state it.

Step 4: Eventually, shift into a mood of perplexity and curiosity with some questions, like:

- Is this really true? Is it an assertion/fact, or an assessment/interpretation? What's some evidence to the contrary?

- *When did this belief form? What was the event, and how did I interpret it at the time?*

- Who am I being when I hold this belief? Is it a perspective of the small self or my greater Spirit Self?

- What do I want/how do I want to feel instead? (shift to outcome frame)

- How else can I think about this? *What would Source say about this? (Spirit perspective)*

- *In a Universe of infinite possibilities, what else is possible? How could this be better?*

Similarly to shifting moods and emotions, there might be layers to work through in shifting a belief. Someone once said that beliefs are like wolves, in that they travel in packs. It's not uncommon that when you find one belief to shift, other related beliefs show up, as well. No worries. Just take it one step at a time. Each step will be a loosening, and you'll feel the difference. And, even if you're not aware of other beliefs, they will eventually show up for you through some physical or emotional response.

Again, the important point in this adaptation of EFT is to shift your story or belief to one held by Spirit, by reminding yourself of any appropriate presuppositions held by Spirit. It might help you to review that list or to have it nearby before you do your tapping.

Sample process and script for shifting a belief of your smaller-self to one of Spirit's perspective

This is an example. The specifics for each person will be different.

Let's say you're experiencing a lot of stress and anxiety at home and work, with an intensity level around 8

To reveal the underlying belief(s) that could be creating this emotional response, you could answer one or more of these questions:

I feel this way because… There's so much to do and I have to get it right/do it perfectly.

What's stopping me from being more relaxed? It's hard to do it all perfectly/exactly as I need and want it to be.

This is a problem because… I can never relax about it, or let it be good enough. I take too long doing things. I'm hard on other people. It's hard to let go at night.

A fear I have about this is… If I don't do things perfectly, there will be negative consequences. I might get fired, or not respected enough at work. People might think less of me (in personal and professional life).

So, there seems to be an underlying belief that if you don't do everything perfectly, there could be negative consequences, and/or people will think less of you. Let's tap on this.

Set up:

Even though I think I have to do everything perfectly, and it creates a lot of stress and anxiety for me, I honor these feelings as guidance from my Soul that there's an opportunity for me to become more of my whole Spirit-Self.

Even though I think I have to do everything perfectly, and it creates a lot of stress and anxiety for me, I honor these feelings as guidance that I'm just being my small self; and I just need to return to my whole, Spirit-Self perspective.

Even though I think I have to do everything perfectly, and it creates a lot of stress and anxiety for me, I love and accept myself as best I can, and am open to letting this go and thinking about things differently.

Now go through the tapping points, stating your automatic thoughts regarding your current belief, and all the thoughts and feelings you have about it:

I have to do things right.

It's important to do things the right way.

Things need to be done perfectly.

Something could happen if I don't, or people might think less of me.

It feels like I have to be perfect, or else.

I'm supposed to be perfect. It's not okay to not be perfect.

And it's tiring! It's hard! I'm always anxious about it. It's there all the time.

Begin to loosen and shift your thinking, with questions, and considering Spirit's perspective:

Maybe these feelings are my Soul trying to tell me something. Maybe what I keep thinking isn't really true.

Maybe it's worth questioning.

It's not really a fact that I have to be perfect, is it? There's not exactly a rule in the world that we have to be perfect and do everything perfectly. I guess I'm just thinking that. I'm making it up.

But it feels so true. How can I trust letting it go?

Maybe there's evidence to the contrary. Now that I think of it, there's lots of evidence to the contrary.

I haven't been perfect many, many times, and it's been okay. More than okay. In many ways. (You can list them.)

When did I learn this belief, this "mistaken" interpretation?

I can recall this same feeling when I was a child. Like thinking I should get A's in school. Like wanting praise from Mom and Dad when I did anything well. Like when I noticed their disappointment if I didn't. And when they scolded me for doing something wrong.

I remember thinking my friends wouldn't like me if I didn't play well on their team.

But nothing bad really happened! Everyone still loved me, and my friends still liked me. It was all in my head!

No one told me there's a rule that everyone has to be perfect. I just came to that conclusion on my own, from my child's mind.

I am a unique extension of Spirit. Spirit created me and intentionally came here as me, *as my unique self*. From Spirit's perspective, there is no perfect. Spirit does not have such impossible conditions, and maybe there's a reason for that. Maybe that's a greater intelligence than I've been coming from!

Maybe there's no such thing as perfect. Maybe it's not what's most important.

I get to choose my standards as contextually appropriate.

Maybe as I relax into my true Self, everything will work out for me. I create as I think and speak.

If I focus on ease and what I want, that's what I'll attract.

Expanding with my breath into my Whole Self feels different! It feels freer. It feels easier. It feels full of love and acceptance.

I'm open to letting my old, mistaken thinking go.

I'm open to letting my feelings remind me when I've forgotten the higher truths, and when I need to take some big breaths and return to my Spirit-Self.

I think and feel so differently as my greater Self.

Thank you, thank you, thank you!

Recap and practice

Tapping is a really useful way to relax your state so that you're able to tell yourself a better feeling, *believable* story, one that shifts you out of being just your smaller self and opens you up to your greater Spirit-Self and the magnificent life that can then open up for you.

Although it doesn't offer the spiritual aspect of tapping, www.thetappingsolution.com is a great resource for becoming more comfortable with tapping in general. It has more videos you can watch; and they also have a phone app with many, many tapping guided meditations. Of course, there's always YouTube, too!

I love tapping so much. I hope you'll play with it and get to experience how beautifully wisdom arises when you relax and settle the small self mind. It will! Spirit's wisdom and guidance are always within you. It's only a matter of being able to access it. ALL of the strategies we've covered in the book are different ways to settle your smaller-self perspective and to return to your Whole, Spirit-Self again. Each strategy a doorway to your Soul.

CHAPTER EIGHT

Putting it all together and next steps

It's time to tie everything together that we've covered, in a way that you can use in your day-to-day, even your moment by moment, as needed. It really can be so simple.

There's no need now to put up with extended periods of not feeling good; and no need to feel at the effect of your emotions or your outer circumstances. You are WAY more than that. If it's your commitment to live more and more from the space and perspective of your infinite Spirit-Self that always has a solution, that always feels love and acceptance, and that has the creative powers to be, do and have all that you desire, then you will live predominantly in a higher vibration and an underlying core of inner peace and joy no matter what, and be delighted on a daily basis with what you manifest, and with life.

Once you've completed your reading of this book, rather than considering it finished or complete, and moving on to a new book, I suggest you continue to focus on these ideas and strategies for a while, and to now consider yourself on a path of mastering what you read about. Aim towards moving to conscious, and then unconscious competence, and from being minimally competent to competent, and then to being a virtuoso, and then eventually to the more free, fun and innovative level of mastery.

I've worked with a lot of people over the years. Sometimes, while still working with me, in their enthusiasm for learning and growth, a client would also sign up for another workshop with someone else, or read some other books. I found that they didn't progress as well as those who just focused on our work while they developed greater competence at it. So, I encourage you to give yourself the gift of time and focus to do the same.

Learning is more than just a once-through of gathering information. It's also *doing*. To nurture this, create a plan that feels good and doable for you for focusing on and practicing aspects of the book each day. For example, you might like to take one chapter a week to review the key points and skills, and to follow the recommendations in each "recap and practice" section. Be sure to review the tips (several times!) for using language effectively and how to tell a better feeling story. These are key to making it easy.

By playing with aspects of the book on a daily basis, you'll be incrementally building your skills and your new neural networks. This new neurology will eventually allow you to use the skills with greater confidence, competence, and ease, and to think in new ways more automatically.

My biggest recommendation is to begin with being committed to being mindful of your Soul's guidance through the doorways of your body and emotions, and to using your power to create through your doorway of language. What stories are you telling that are creating how you feel? If they don't feel good and don't support you, change them! Don't listen to the "static", right? To help reinforce this commitment and to set your inner "GPS", I suggest setting this intention as you awaken. If it feels easier, begin with a simple morning intention with just one or two intentions; and then adjust and build as you feel inclined to do so.

So, to start, you might begin your morning with something like, "It's my ongoing intention to be mindful of how I feel physically and emotionally. If at any time I don't feel good, I will notice what story I'm telling myself, take some centering breaths to "re-Source" and remember who I truly am, and to shift my story to one that better supports what I want and my Spirit's perspective."

To have the Spirit presuppositions ready at hand when needed, I suggest reviewing the summary list or slides every day. Perhaps read them with your morning cup of coffee, or before your morning intentions or meditation, or even as a meditation! Or have them in the bathroom for good reading! Create a habit that works for you, until you no longer need it anymore.

Here are the basic steps you can take when you don't like how you're feeling at any point during your day, in any moment. It's just creating a shift in thinking.

"I don't like how I'm feeling. What do I do?"

1. Remember that any emotion (desirable or undesirable) is a response to your inner narrative. So, if you don't feel good, *get the story out!* Ask yourself, "What am I thinking that's creating this feeling?" or "I'm feeling this way because..."

    Just asking those questions is usually enough to reveal what's creating how you feel. If, on the odd occasion it's unclear, or too intense, take a few moments to tap. "I don't like how I'm feeling, but I don't know why, yet. I wonder what I'm thinking." Just free associate your thoughts and feelings, and the story will reveal itself. It's definitely there.

2. *Breathe*, center, and relax. This is usually enough to create an adequate, relaxed opening for the next step. If not, again, tapping, even without words, can help, if needed.

3. Shift into curiosity/perplexity. Be open, and begin asking questions. Again, it can be very helpful to tap while doing this; but it's usually not necessary.

- Are these thoughts facts, or just my interpretation?
- What interpretations and meanings am I creating here?
- Shift out of the problem frame, into the outcome frame, asking, "So, what DO I want? *How do I want to feel?*" When thinking about this, it's important to focus on what's in your locus of control, rather than trying to change someone or the outer circumstances. This is about what you are going to change within yourself.
- Who am I being? (small self, or greater Whole, Spirit-Self)

4. If you can, using your own strategy for feeling Spirit, "Re-Source". Expand into the space of Spirit, of love, peace, and pure potential. You can also do this by connecting to your heart.

5. Ask questions like these to change your inner story:
   - What's another possible interpretation/perspective that would feel better and be more useful?
   - How can this be even better? What else is possible?
   - *Consider the presuppositions of Spirit, as well. What would Source/Spirit/my heart say?*

6. Shift your story/inner narrative to a better-feeling, *and <u>believable</u>* one, and to Spirit perspective. (You can refer to Chapter Six, to review this.)

7. IF you're still not able to do that, pick a strategy that feels best to continue:
   Options (in no particular order):
   - Shift your body: your posture, smile, breathe more fully, move, go outside, etc.
   - Meditate (can also use meditation music to help, like Solfeggio frequency music available on YouTube). This can simply mean allowing yourself some time in stillness and quiet.

- Shift into heart coherence and ask for guidance for a more effective response and perspective. Enjoy the feelings of love, gratitude, and joy that the heart coherence process creates.
- EFT/tapping

The purpose of all the strategies you now have available to you is to shift your story to a more believable, better-feeling, more effective inner narrative/story. In my opinion and experience, incorporating Spirit perspectives can be a most powerful addition, and will help you to live a more enlightened life as your Spirit-Self.

"Abracadabra! (I create as I speak!) It is done!"

Create and use easy, daily habits of using your strategies preventatively, and to create and maintain a feeling-good, resourceful, Spirit-Self way of being:

- When you awaken, speak your morning intentions for who and how you want to be

- Meditate (you have many strategies now), even if just for a few minutes, even if it's just sitting in stillness for a few minutes. You want to reconnect to your Whole Self.

- Begin and/or end your day with gratitude and remembering what's good and what's right in your world.

- Practice mindfulness. *Notice when you don't feel good, physically or emotionally, and don't put up with that "static"!* Follow the steps above right away, even if it's just tapping on your karate chop points.

- Make it a point to breathe and center regularly throughout your day, and to take care of your body.

- End your day with some kind of *intentional* self-care/pleasure.

Whether it's having a cup of tea or watching something good on TV (actually find something you'll enjoy) or reading, doing so *intentionally acknowledging* it as your reward for the day and as time to relax, can make a big difference in the positive effect it will have for you. As you reflect on what you can be grateful for from your day, include acknowledging yourself for what you DID accomplish, and anything you can feel good about, whether big or small. This approach to ending your day can make a huge difference in emotional balance.

- Throughout your day, or, at the very least at the end of your day, acknowledge the strategies you used and take notice of how they worked for you. There is no such thing as failure, only feedback! Most likely, you will have experienced a positive result; and acknowledging this helps to reinforce future use of the strategies.

- And, HAVE FUN LEARNING! *Practice makes progress!*

Below is a guided tapping meditation integrating and reviewing everything we've covered; so it's a great way to review, reinforce, and "wire in" the important concepts in the book. It has reminders to help you create and experience more inner peace, love, ease, and joy, by living from your greater Spirit-Self perspective. It's about 20 minutes. I suggest tapping along as the best choice to help get it into your neurology; but if you get a little tired of tapping, I think it's still valuable to listen to in a meditative, or even a non-meditative state. I've also included a copy of the script I used, in case you'd also like to read it. Using either of these can support you in remembering and embodying the strategies and concepts in the book.

To listen to a guided tapping meditation integrating and reviewing everything we've covered, go to www.new possibilitiescoaching.com/three-doorways-to-the-soul-book .html.

Tapping integration and review script:

Start with three deep breaths, inhale, exhale.

Begin with the eyebrow point, and *move to the next point with each phrase.*

Learning is a process.

I appreciate all that I'm learning, and that I'm getting better and better at remembering that I am Spirit, having this human experience. Somehow, I know this in my heart.

It's an ongoing process. Of being mindful of how I feel, and what my emotional guidance is telling me.

I am the creator of my experience through my thoughts. Knowing I have that power feels good!

I create as I speak – Abracadabra!

The quality of my life depends on the quality of the conversations I have with myself.

I choose to be mindful of my thoughts.

I can choose how I feel by choosing the interpretations I make and the inner stories I tell myself.

Nothing has meaning other than the meaning I attach to it. I get to choose. There is no one truth or reality.

My feelings and emotions do not have to be at the effect of others or outer circumstances. I can choose my own interpretation, and I choose one that feels better. Spirit perspective always feels good.

My emotions are not a response to reality. They are a response to the story I am creating.

My feelings are an indicator of what kind of story I'm telling, and remind me of when to be mindful, and that I'm holding a belief or telling myself a story that isn't necessarily true and doesn't serve me, and is not aligned with Source perspective.

If I don't like how I'm feeling, the first step is to ask myself, "What am I thinking that's creating this feeling?" or "I'm feeling this way because..."

Then I can breathe, center, and relax, and continue to ask more questions.

I can shift out of the problem frame, into the outcome frame, asking, "So, what DO I want?"

I can ask "Who am I being?" (small self, or greater Whole, Spirit-Self) And I can use my association for feeling Spirit to Re-Source, and expand into the space of Spirit, of Love, peace, and pure potential.

I can ask, "Is this really true, or just my interpretation? What interpretation would feel better?

What would Source say?"

I am not my thoughts. I simply have thoughts. I choose to be curious about my thoughts rather than judge them.

I enjoy living in a state of perplexity or wonder, rather than knowing, including about other people.

Breathing fully from my belly feels good, and helps me stay calm and centered.

I will pause regularly throughout the day and ask myself, "How am I feeling?" and will center and breathe and renew myself as needed.

My body also alerts me to who I'm being and how I'm vibrating. I can easily shift my body to shift my state: like with my posture, intentionally smiling, breathing more fully, moving, and going outside.

Meditating feels so good. I have so many different ways I can meditate to make it easy and pleasurable.

I can focus on the simplicity and beauty of my breath and the flow of Spirit through me.

I can simply imagine how I will feel when my desire is fulfilled and why I want it.

I can fully recall positive memories, or visualize any representations or symbols of how I want to feel.

I can focus on gratitude.

I can state what I'm open and willing to, or what I'm the space for.

I can focus on the space of stillness and quiet that already exists.

I can imagine and step into a different perspective.

I can connect to my heart for wisdom and guidance.

I can repeat simple mantras that feel good, like love, peace, calm, thank you, or I am here.

Meditating is a way to practice being mindful and aware of my thoughts, and choosing good ones.

I focus on what I want instead of what I don't want; and use language that directs me to where I want to go. I have my own inner GPS system.

Given the unique mental maps or programs they have, people are always making the best, perceive choice available to them. Including me.

A computer can only work as well as it's programmed. It's the same with people.

Behind every behavior and reaction is a positive intention, a part trying to take care of an important concern, even when it may not seem that way. When I honor the intention and that caring part, I can just try a more effective strategy.

When I address the underlying intentions of myself and others, I can find a win-win for all.

There is no such thing as failure, only feedback.

Every experience and problem I have can be a gift and opportunity for learning and growth, and to become more and more of my highest, best self. Life happens FOR me, not to me.

I will remember to see myself and others through the eyes of Source.

I choose to be open and willing to the changes I desire. I am the space for all possibilities.

The space of stillness and peace is always available to me. I just have to focus on where it already exists, even if it's outside in the space around me. It's right there.

I am not my beliefs. I am the creator of my beliefs, and thus the creator of my life.

I choose to argue against my limiting beliefs instead of for them.

I can find evidence to the contrary of my beliefs, and evidence that supports my desired belief.

I am SO much more than my body.

I choose to use the power of my intentions.

I can tap my way to however I want to feel. The magic in my fingertips is always available to me. I can even just tap without any words.

I am Spirit, and I have a body.

Source/Spirit is the creator of everything, and I am an extension of Source. Therefore, I am a creator; and I have all I need within me.

Because I exist in an infinite field of pure potentiality, unlimited abundance and possibilities for accomplishing the essence of any desired outcome are available to all, including me.

Uncertainty = unlimited possibilities are still available.

As I'm open to uncertainty and let go of attachment and knowing, I keep all possibilities open and available to me.

If I can imagine it, I can be, do, or have anything I desire.

I am responsible for my experience. Everything I experience is a reflection of my vibration and focus, and what I have thus created.

"Ask and you shall receive." Inherent within every intention and desire are the mechanics for their fulfillment. When I have a desire, the way for the essence of my desire to manifest exists, and it puts the infinite, organizing power of the Universe to work for me. The field of potential takes form in a vibrational reality, and "It is done!" (the essence of the desire/why it is wanted, is done) It will manifest in a physical form available to my senses when I tune in to the frequency of that vibrational reality, like tuning into a radio station.

I allow others their experience, because as Source/Spirit, there is no right or wrong. Everything just is.

Through their thought and focus and attention, everyone is a creator of their reality, and they are all valid. Because from Source-perspective, there is no one truth. It is an all-inclusive Universe.

There is only a source of well-being. I either allow it or not.

Contrast, diversity, and polarities are all part of the process of creation, growth, and evolution (personally and collectively). Therefore, I can accept and even appreciate all of it. All is well from this perspective.

Spirit is love-based. Everyone is perfect, worthy, and lovable as they are, including me. It is a given.

Behind every behavior is a positive intention, no matter how evil, crazy or bizarre it seems.

People, including me, always make the best choice they perceive as available to them, according to the conditioned programs they exist from.

When you know better/differently, you do better/differently.

The Universe operates through dynamic exchange. Energy needs to flow. As we give, we receive. There will always be an ebb and flow.

Source/Nature's intelligence functions with effortless ease. Therefore, when I am aligned with Source, in states of harmony, love, and joy, I can accomplish what I want with ease.

I can never get it wrong and I will never get it done; because I am an eternal being, and I can create newly in every moment. There is no failure. It is only feedback for more learning and growth.

Life is supposed to be FUN! The basis of life is freedom. The purpose of life is JOY. And the result of the perfect combination of the two is motion forward and growth. I am a creator, and the subject of my creation is my joyful life experience. That is my mission. That is my quest. That is why I am here.

There is no death. I am an eternal being. The body dies, but the energy does not. Energy is eternal. It cannot be destroyed, only transformed. When the body dies, the energy transitions to pure Spirit essence again, and is available to those still living.

Spirit will never lower its vibration to match a lower perspective of mine or another. When an emotion doesn't feel good, it's an indicator of the gap between the perspective I'm holding as a mere human self and the perspective of my greater Spirit-Self. I'm feeling the incongruity.

The more I use my strategies and use the perspective of my greater Spirit Self, the better and better I feel.

I'm capable of more than I thought.

Feeling good is easier than I imagined.

I am (insert your name here), and so much more.

And so it is.

Thank you, thank you, thank you!

I hope you will continue to have FUN with this process of learning and expansion, with engaging in the magic and fun of living as a deliberate creator and your life getting better and better, and appreciating the gifts in *every* aspect of being Spirit in these amazing bodies!

One last thing: As is happening with more and more people on the planet these days, I wrote this book because I felt a very strong spiritual calling to do so. I did not write it to generate business or to make money. I truly just want this content and these strategies to be easily accessible to people, because I know what a huge positive difference it can make for those who practice it, and the positive ripple effect that can have. I want more and more people to be happy!

This is why I am freely sharing it, and ask you to freely share it, as well. Who do you know that would appreciate this book? Please let them know about it. It will be available for free here: www.newpossibilities coaching.com/three-doorways-to-the-soul-book.html.

Please leave a review on Amazon when you're done, as that will help with my mission, as well! Thank you!

I'd love to hear from you! You can email me at annide@newpossibilitiescoaching.com.

About The Author

Since the mid-'80s, Ann has been helping people experience more inner peace and joy through her private and group New Possibilities Coaching programs, and her guided meditation classes. She was also a trainer for the NLP (Neurolinguistic Programming) practitioner-level course for the Massachusetts Institute of NLP.

Ann also taught at Boston College for 10 years, working with high-risk students. At that time, she was also training college faculty and staff nationally in Learning to Learn, a proven methodology for improving learning effectiveness.

She received her Master's level certification and a Master's degree in Neurolinguistic Programming and Hypnotherapy, and trained and mentored under a number of the developers and masters of NLP. Since then, she also became certified as an NLP life coach.

Other than her passion for helping people, her other greatest passion is being outdoors in nature, and spending as much time as possible by the ocean, in the woods, hiking, biking, and kayaking.

She started New Possibilities Coaching with her husband, Mark, and they continue to share their passion for helping people live their lives more from their Spirit-Selves' perspective. Their website is:

www.NewPossibilitiesCoaching.com

You can email Ann at annide@newpossibilitiescoaching.com.

www.ingramcontent.com/pod-product-compliance
Lightning Source LLC
Chambersburg PA
CBHW061318040426
42444CB00011B/2704